Mark Olsen 3/81

Mark Olsen 3/81

The book of the
DRAGON

Silene.

fua anno Vtolans

aput viuente Sige

punteta huc aduenisti: vel quo   imortalis dei impio deseruire. se in
nomine vateris. Sanctus ge   aciauus dixit. Eras
orgius dixit. Xpianus † dei   grorgi: aeede † im
seruus sum: erequus nimia   nole dei applin

The book of the
DRAGON

Judy Allen & Jeanne Griffiths

CHARTWELL BOOKS INC.

To the founder members of the Garnstone Press

Title page: *The story of St George, told here in full on this breviary painted
for the Duke of Bedford in the fifteenth century. In the foreground the
Princess leads the dragon back to the people before St George finally kills
him.*

Acknowledgments

The publishers would like to acknowledge the help of the following museums,
private collections and individuals in permitting the reproduction of the
photography shown on the pages listed:

Julian Barnard: page 126 top. Berthelot Collection, Venice: page 10 top.
Bibliothèque Nationale, Paris: pages 2, 35, 77, 79, 124. Bodleian Library,
Oxford: pages 15, 33 top, 46, 49, 51, 55, 67, 114 bottom, 115 top right, 117. By
courtesy of the Trustees of the British Museum: pages 8, 11, 14 bottom, 16, 17,
19 top, 19 left, 20, 21, 23, 26, 28, 30, 34, 54, 57, 58 top, 58 bottom, 61, 65, 66, 70
top, 70 right, 71, 72, 73, 75, 78, 81, 82, 83, 107, 112 top, 113, 115 top left, 122, 123,
125. Cairo Museum, 126 bottom, Bruce Coleman Ltd: Pages 91, 94 top, 94
bottom, 95. Etruscan Museum, Vatican: page 32. Jeff Foot: page 91. Werner
Forman: pages 9, 10 bottom, 14 top, 38, 40, 45, 50 top, 58 top, 58 bottom, 59, 63,
102, 111 top, 126 bottom. G. B. Frith: page 94 top. Gulbenkian Museum of
Oriental Arts, Durham: pages 36, 39, 42. Sonia Halliday: pages 47, 103. The
Hamlyn Group: page 22. William Heinemann: page 99. Michael Holford: pages
43, 123. Keystone Press Agency: page 62 top. Lambeth Palace Library, London: page
100. Mary Evans Picture Library, London: page 64. Metropolitan Museum of
Art, New York: page 84. Musée Guimet, Paris: page 45. Musée du Louvre,
Paris: pages 22, 31. Museum of Ethnology, Berlin: page 59. National Gallery,
London: pages 110, 111 bottom, 118. National Maritime Museum, Greenwich:
pages 65, 85. Goetz D. Plage: page 94 bottom. Scala, Florence: page 7.
Shakespeare Centre, Stratford: page 87. Staatliche Museum, Berlin: page 18.
Stampe Storiche, Milan: pages 88, 93. Statens Historiska Museum, Stockholm:
page 102. Tate Gallery, London: pages 112 bottom, 120. Uffizi Gallery,
Florence: page 7. Universitetets Oldsaksamling, Oslo: 50 right, 101. Victoria &
Albert Museum, London: pages 12, 43, 44, 48, 56, 111 top, 121. Viking Ships
Museum, Oslo: page 50 top. Roger Viollet: page 31. The Vorpal Galleries, San
Francisco: page 109. The Wallace Collection, London: page 116. John Webb:
page 105.

The authors would like to extend their special thanks to Rev Anthony Duncan,
Anoushka Faroughy, Dr Hassal and his colleagues at the Bodleian Library,
Research Reports, Patrick Rudd, Harry Shepperd, and Ian Stewart-Hargreaves.

Contents

Introduction 7

The Cosmic Serpent 8

The First Dragons 17

Classical Dragons 25

Eastern Dragons 34

Western Dragons 46

Plumed Serpents and Lake Monsters 57

Dragons in Alchemy and Psychology 67

Dragons on Maps 78

Dragons in Zoology 86

Dragons in Epic and Folklore 98

Dragons in Art and Heraldry 109

Slaying the Dragon 118

Bibliography 127

Index 128

Introduction

The dragon drifts his way through the art and mythology of the ancient and modern worlds like a recurring dream. And, dream-like, his forms and attributes change, from East to West and from age to age.

There are no such things as dragons. Yet the dragon as a symbol has been used by virtually every culture throughout the history of the world. Most mythologies agree that he was born of clouds and water. Like them he is everywhere, and his appearance is as mutable as theirs.

He is probably the most fluid of fabulous beasts, in every sense. Yet despite this, or perhaps because of it, he is everywhere. He appears in creation myths and nightmares, devouring virgins and in combat with heroes, giving knowledge and stealing knowledge, withholding rain and granting rain, pursuing the sacred pearl and guarding a secret treasure; in religious books and children's stories, in works of art and science, in paintings and drawings, on porcelain, in wood, in gold, on paper; in most countries of the world and at most stages of their history.

The dragon has immense power as a symbol and yet remains nebulous in form and meaning. Compiling a book on dragons is rather like taking on one of the impossible tasks of epic legend; pursuing him through libraries and museums seems to parallel more ancient pursuits across deserts and up mountains! It is almost as if he retains his potency through preserving his privacy. Get in close and he floats away elsewhere, look directly at him and he shifts his shape as clouds or mist shift theirs. Eventually it becomes almost possible to believe that the dragon deeply resents this attempt at a form of capture and that simple evasion may turn into some form of vengeance.

Dissect a flower and the beauty and magic of it are lost. But, do what you will, the beauty and magic of the dragon remain safe. It is no more possible to find the definitive dragon than it would be to frame a cloud formation. The survey of dragons which follows shows him in his various aspects and humours, as seen and interpreted by various people throughout history, offers a few definitions and a lot of pictures, but does not attempt to constrain or constrict something which is at once as constant and as changeable as the spirit of a people or a place.

Above *The story of Perseus and Andromeda is here told in a painting by Piero di Cosimo. Perseus sees the maiden chained to a rock and on hearing the story from her anxious parents, he slays the dragon in return for the maiden's hand in marriage.*

The Cosmic Dragon

Above *A papyrus of Padiu-Khous shows the deceased offering a heart to the winged serpent.*

To define a dragon it seems necessary to steal Antony's description of a crocodile from Shakespeare's *Antony and Cleopatra*: 'It is shaped, sir, like itself; and it is as broad as it hath breadth; it is just so high as it is, and moves with its own organs; it lives by that which nourisheth it; and the elements once out of it, it transmigrates.'

The Encyclopaedia Britannica is clearer on the subject, pointing out that the word 'dragon' is derived 'through the French and Latin from the Greek *drakon*, connected with *derkomai* "see", and interpreted as sharp-sighted. The equivalent English word "drake" or "fire-drake" is derived from Anglo-Saxon *draca*. In Greece the word *drakon* was used originally of any large serpent, and the dragon of mythology, whatever shape it may have assumed, remains essentially a snake.'

There is no doubt that, in the earliest forms which are available to us, dragon and serpent mythology were closely interwoven. A few archetypal symbols seem to be common to most of humanity, and three of these – the sacred or cosmic serpent, the celestial tree and the dragon – appear either together or separately all over the world. In later mythology the dragon and the snake separate – the dragon becoming more complex, both physically and spiritually – yet even in relatively recent medieval stories, in which local dragons were put to death by local dignitaries, it is sometimes referred to as a 'Worme'.

It is interesting to consider whether the serpent was gradually elaborated into a dragon, or whether the one-time dragon degenerated into a serpent, whose past glory is sometimes remembered in dragon legends. Surprisingly enough, the suggestion that the ancient dragon may have degenerated into a snake, rather than the other way around, is at least a possibility. In his book *The Dragons of Eden*, Dr Carl Sagan says: 'Snakes have evolved from four-legged reptilian ancestors resembling dragons. Many snakes still retain anatomical vestiges of the limbs of their ancestors.' A third alternative is that, mythologically, dragons and snakes are cousins in whom the family likeness is so strong that they are sometimes confused with each other.

Whatever may be the true explanation, it is not possible to ignore either the great cosmic serpent of the primitive creation myths, or the ubiquitous serpent-worship of the ancient world, both of which are closely connected with the first dragons. Most cultures have formed or adapted creation myths in which the cosmic serpent or dragon played a vital role. The ancient cosmic serpent, who shared so many of his attributes with the dragon, had more than one function. R.T. Rundle Clark in *Myth and Symbol in Ancient Egypt* says: (apart from the proper names, this list is relevant not only to Egypt but to most of the rest of the world as well)

The major symbolic activities of the male serpent are: 1) as creator or most ancient manifestation of the emergent spirit; 2) as a monster which has to be overcome before the world can be said to be really in order; 3) as Sito, a serpent-god who encircles the world, either with many coils, or with its tail in its mouth, or walking – with legs provided! 4) as the spirit or guardian of the earth or underworld; 5) as cosmic enemy, the serpent-dragon Apophis, who personifies the powers of darkness and has to be overcome at dawn and sunset; 6) as fertility spirit – chiefly in the form of the corn-god; 7) as water-god, especially living in caverns out of which the Nile flood was believed to come; 8) as a distinguishing form of the non-human – the serpent is a primeval creature, living in the dark earth or the depths of the water [the eel?], uncanny and hostile – and, possibly, very wise.

As creator or creatrix, (the serpent-dragon was sometimes female), this creative element was sometimes also identified with the chaos which had to be overcome for the world to be properly ordered. As spirit or guardian of the earth it manifested in various ways – as Python, the oracular serpent at Delphi, or as the hoard-guarding dragon of epic and folklore. As cosmic enemy, the serpent-dragon appears in conflict with the solar hero. As fertility spirit or corn-god he appears, rather disguised, in conflict with the reaper as St George; as water-god he appears as Hydra in Greek mythology and Naga in Indian mythology, and in his 'distinguishing form of the non-human' he appears everywhere. It is only as encircler of the earth that he is wholly serpent.

The encircler of the earth, the great snake which lies coiled, tail in mouth, around the world appears under many names and is closely connected with the 'monster who kept back the waters'. All aspects of the cosmic serpent overlap, and Apophis, probably an early Egyptian solar god, appears sometimes as encircler of the earth and sometimes as cosmic enemy. Here, as everywhere, the ambivalent nature of the creature is apparent. Apophis holds the earth together, preventing it from flying into bits as it spins through space, but also he longs to break free and destroy it. In all the major dragon-serpent symbols the good and the bad are delicately balanced.

Left *The sun-god Re is drawn in the Evening Boat through the Realms of Night. The serpent Mehen protects him from the serpent Apep who seeks to destroy him. The idea of a serpent destroying the sun every night also occurs in South America and Burma (from the Valley of Kings at Thebes).*

The encircler of the earth is associated with the cosmic ocean. Primitive cosmologies taught that the world was surrounded by water which fertilized it in the form of rain but which also threatened flood and destruction. The monster, or serpent, who held back these waters was protecting the earth from inundation, but he was also capable of causing drought. Horapollo, a Ptolemaic writer, says that the Egyptians represented the universe as a serpent devouring its tail. In Rabbinic belief, Leviathan was coiled around the earth. He girdled the earth – its creator, protector and potential destroyer. The mountains were his dung, earthquakes were caused by his restless movements and the world was in constant danger that if his hunger grew too great he would devour it and destroy it.

Gnostic gems often depict this tail-biter, as do alchemical scrolls. In the *Elder Edda*, an Icelandic poetic manuscript written in the thirteenth century, the Midgard Snake encircles Midgard, the known world. In the earliest sacred writings of Persia it is stated that Trita smote Azhi, a primeval dragon, before Indra killed 'the monster that kept back the waters'. In the *Rig Veda*, a collection of Sanskrit hymns dating from about 1000 BC, the monster is the demon of drought, which is why he is slain by Indra, sometimes known as the lord of the storm.

In Central and South American mythology 'the monster that kept back the waters' is represented as a snake and is shown in the company of the elephant-headed rain god. The Maya Codex Troana shows the elephant-headed god Chac standing on the head of a serpent as he himself pours

Above The Dragon appears as the tail-biting Ouroboros in the eleventh-century Codex Marcianus. The Ouroboros was the earliest alchemical symbol.

Below Carved Nagas, or god snakes, guard this Hindu shrine at Tampaksiring in Bali.

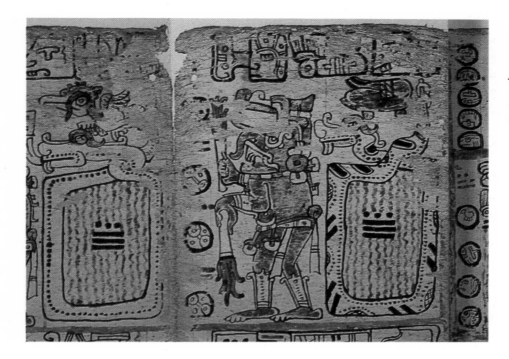

water to the earth. In the Codex Cortes, the serpent, is clearly seen to be restraining or holding back the waters. Professor G. Elliot Smith, in *The Evolution of the Dragon*, (1919) says:

> The serpent (the American rattlesnake) restrains the water by coiling itself into a sac to hold up the rain and so prevent it from reaching the earth. In the various American codices this episode is depicted in as great a variety of forms as the Vedic poets of India described when they sang of the exploits of Indra. The Maya Chac is, in fact, Indra transferred to the other side of the Pacific and there only thinly disguised by a veneer of American stylistic design.

The cosmic serpent was worshipped in his earthly form and there are certain important symbolic attributes which are common both to snakes and dragons – their close connection with water, their reputed possession of a fabulous or priceless jewel or treasure, their sharp sight, their wisdom and their uncertain temper. Even in cultures which worshipped the snake with every sign of love rather than fear, the absolute necessity of housing it well, bringing it gifts, and performing the correct rituals was a tacit admission that it was moody and that its benevolence had to be sought or bought.

Both are also connected with immortality – they either possess it, or can confer it, sometimes both. It has often been suggested that one of the reasons that the snake, in particular, attracted more reverence than any other living creature was because it was seen to shed its skin and emerge slightly larger and infinitely brighter than before. This led to the belief that the snake died but was reborn, and had therefore conquered death. It is possible that this in turn led to the belief that the snake was all-wise. One of mankind's earliest obsessions was the possibility of avoiding old age and death, and the snake's apparent mastery of this led to its widespread use in funeral rites in the hope that it would pass on the information at the appropriate time.

11

Above *The serpent often appears in association with evil, here with a Sinhalese demon figure. This was perhaps because most serpents were considered deadly poisonous.*

Below *Buddha seated on the folds of a great Naga which protects him with its inner hood of 7 folds, and outer hood of 14 folds. This figure is one of the sculptures of the Buddhist stupas at Amravati in India.*

The snake in particular was commonly connected with death, with resurrection and with fertility. With death because it was found underneath stones, in the roots of trees and in caverns and crevices in the ground and was therefore taken to be the spirit of the earth, of the underworld, the chthonic numen of the tree; with resurrection because of its ability to shed its skin and be reborn; with fertility because it was the spirit of fertilizing water, of springs which came from underground, and of rain, and because slipping into the earth's crevices as it did it was believed to impregnate the great mother. It was believed to guard the hidden treasures of the earth, especially the precious metals that could be mined from it, and this was extended into the belief that it was greedy for treasure and that valuable gifts should be brought to sacred snakes in captivity. Because of its swift and zig-zag movements it was associated with lightning and with the hoard of gold that was believed in some cultures to form at the base of the lightning's strike. And it was believed to have the power of healing, partly because of its presumed immortality and partly because the venom in the bite of a snake could only be neutralized with serum made from the same venom.

Serpent worship is widespread and extraordinarily similar in form in different parts of the world. Often it is not, in a sense, the living snake itself which is worshipped, but the god that the snake represents. In *Tree and Serpent Worship*, J. Fergusson says that the serpent cult appears to have originated among the Turanian peoples of the Lower Euphrates and to have spread throughout the old world wherever the Turanians settled. In *The Migration of Early Culture*, G. Elliot Smith suggests that it originated in Egypt about 800 BC and was spread by the Phoenicians to India, the Far East and the Pacific Islands, from whence it eventually reached America. It is not within the scope of this book to suggest by what route or from which peoples these ideas might have travelled – or even if they travelled at all, since it is still considered probable that, despite their similarity, they might have sprung up independently – but it is interesting to consider just a few of the places where it has been found, and a few of the forms it has taken. A brief and scattered sampling can give an indication of the immense range and the immense power of the cult.

Serpent-worship flourished throughout Africa, and to a certain extent still exists there – which is hardly surprising for a continent with so many snakes. The serpent cult at Whidah in Dahomey, which has been catalogued in detail, was typical of cults in other parts of West Africa. Here there were three groups of gods – Serpents, Trees and the Ocean – and Dan gbwe, the earth serpent, was principal among these. There was also the heavenly serpent, or Dan Ayido Hwedo, which appeared as the rainbow. These great snakes were represented either by a coiled and horned clay snake within a calabash, or by a live python. The great and immortal python was kept in a temple or snake house, with many other snakes, but he himself was only visible to the priests, although the king was allowed to see him once in his lifetime. The python was almighty, omniscient and oracular and was prayed and sacrificed to and given gifts. He had a thousand snake wives, or priestesses, who had either been given to the god at birth and brought up in the temple or had been 'chosen' by him later. Any girl or woman overcome by hysteria was said to have been chosen, or touched, by the great python. She would be taken for a while into a special hospital and then, having been tattooed with the image of the god like the other snake wives, would be returned to normal life but ever afterwards regarded as a fetish woman. Immense human sacrifices were made, but these seem to have been intended to supply past and dead kings with an adequate court rather than to feed the snake.

In Fiji the supreme god Ndengei was thought to take the form of a vast serpent. A snake was kept in his shrine and fed by a priest, occasionally with human victims. Again he was omniscient and oracular and he controlled the rainfall and received the gifts and prayers of the people.

In North and South America the serpent was very powerful. To many of the tribes of North American Indians he was a rain-serpent who would permit drought if not suitably propitiated with gifts. To the Indians of South America he was the mighty Quetzalcoatl or plumed serpent. In Mexico rattlesnakes were kept in temples and fed on the flesh of human sacrifices. In Central America human victims were offered to a living serpent-god by the Zacatec Indians. In Peru the pre-Inca race venerated serpents and offered human hearts and blood to them, and later the Incas kept snakes in temples as sacred creatures.

In India there was a multiplicity of serpent cults, the greatest of which was the worship of the Naga or cobra; sometimes in snake form, sometimes in semi-human form, and sometimes in wholly human form with snake-like appendages or attendants. The Naga and its importance travelled from India to China together with Buddhism.

In Japan some divinities assumed serpent form and specific snakes were sacred to them. Here the living snakes were regarded rather as the servants or confidantes of the deity than as the deity himself.

In Crete excavations have uncovered images of a goddess with snakes twisted around her body and head-dress, accompanied by images of votaries holding snakes who dance before her. In Greece serpents delivered oracles and formed a vital part of the Mystery Cults and of their mythological background.

In Egypt Geb, god of the earth, was 'master of snakes' and had a serpent's head, and the cobra or asp was the symbol of fire and of the solar disc and was therefore worn on the forehead of solar gods and of kings. Despite the fact that the great serpent Apophis was the cosmic enemy of the sun king, the sun god was sometimes represented as a double asp and snakes were highly regarded.

In Italy there are traces of serpent worship at Lanuvium near Rome where a giant serpent supposedly lived in a cave and pronounced judgement on the chastity of the local virgins and on the quality of the harvest to come. If he accepted the offerings brought by the girls he acknowledged their chastity and promised a good harvest – if he refused the offerings both purity and plenty were put in doubt.

A white serpent is king of all the snakes in Celtic lore and Celtic god-images often hold snakes in their hands. William Stukeley suggested that the serpent-shaped mounds found in connection with Stonehenge and Avebury in Britain may indicate serpent-worship, although this has not been proved, and the same is said of the so-called serpent mounds in North America. Serpents were also regarded as important symbols of fertility and prosperity in places as far apart as Australia and Russia.

The connection between snakes and springs, wells and pools is also widespread. Hottentot myths hold that fountains contain snakes; Arab belief associates the snake with medicinal waters; in Greek myth the

Below *In Egyptian mythology the crocodile was worshipped, deified under the name of Sebek. When the canals dried up, this destructive beast roamed the countryside killing and eating, and the Egyptians therefore regarded it as the personification of the powers of evil and death.*

dragon guards the well of Ares, god of war; the dragon of St George had taken over the local spring at Lydda; in North America the snakes live in lakes or pools; Indian Nagas live by water, frequently under trees. The connection between snakes and trees is equally consistent. Not only do Nagas live under trees; in Norse mythology the Midgard Serpent lay coiled at the foot of the sacred ash, the celestial tree, gnawing at its roots, until flung into the waters by Wotan. In North America he was found in the roots of trees struck by lightning, which is why he was thought to be born of the lightning; in Africa serpent and tree worship was interconnected; snakes lived in sacred groves in Greek and Celtic mythology, and so on.

In the West, the best known serpent story is in the creation myth told in Genesis. Serpents or dragons are almost wholly reviled in the Bible and it has been suggested that this powerful attack on them was intended to wipe out established serpent-worship, and that much later images of saints conquering paganism in the specific form of a dragon or snake stem from this. It is possible that the Hebrew brazen serpent was a very early image, connected with healing, which, if not actually worshipped, was at least reverenced until the days of Hezekiah (r.715–686 BC), who destroyed it (II Kings XVIII, 4); an indication that until the time of Hezekiah serpent-worship had not been entirely obliterated. In Christianity, only the Gnostics regarded the snake with favour.

The serpent of Eden continues the snake and tree association, but Sir James Frazer in *Folklore in the Old Testament*, points out that there were

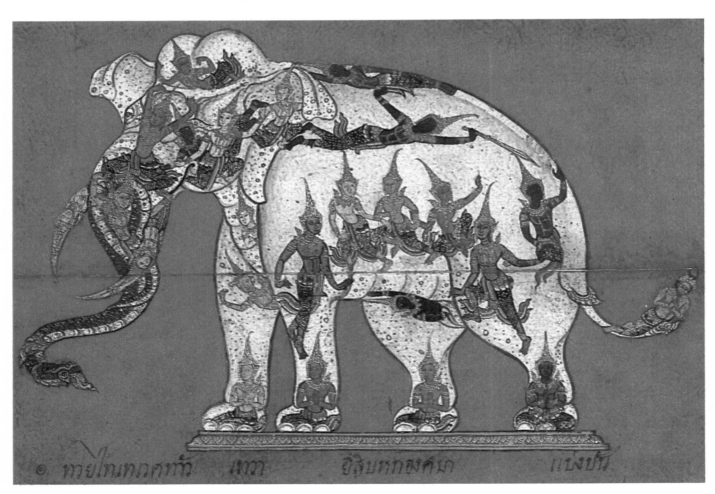

Left The serpent of the Garden of Eden was sometimes depicted as a dragon, or as a serpent with dragon attributes. The words 'serpent' and 'dragon' are interchangeable in the Bible.

two trees in Eden, only one of which really reached prominence in Genesis. In the standard version we are told that there was the Tree of Life and the Tree of the Knowledge of Good and Evil. It is the second tree, the one that was expressly forbidden to man, which appears in all the pictorial representations of the Fall. Man was told that he might eat of any other tree in the garden – therefore he had the opportunity of eating of the Tree of Life and achieving immortality. Frazer suggests that perhaps, originally, the forbidden tree was not of 'knowledge' but of 'death', and that the serpent, symbolizing the underworld, persuaded man to eat of it and then, himself, ate of the Tree of Life. When man was banished from Eden the Tree of Life was automatically barred to him, he had chosen death and the choice was irrevocable. Others, regarding the tree in its form as described in Genesis, as a tree of knowledge, have suggested that by offering this forbidden fruit the serpent deflected man's attention from the Tree of Life, and then ate its fruit himself. Either way, the serpent stole immortality from man, and many mythologies include the theme of man trying to regain from the serpent that which originally he lost to him.

The evil genius of the garden is usually called snake – although Talmudic myth says that it was actually Lillith, first wife of Adam, who was changed into a snake in which form she gave to Eve the secret of the procreation of human life. Lillith is now a Semitic demon, a spirit of the storm and the wilderness, who is particularly spiteful towards children and pregnant women. Alternatively, in the mythology of the serpent and the tree, the serpent is very often the symbol of male sexuality and the tree of female sexuality. Bearing that idea in mind it is possible to see Adam and Eve as the personifications of the symbols, and to understand why the phallic serpent should, having destroyed Eve's innocence, offer to her a symbol of fruitfulness.

Nevertheless, there is some evidence to suggest that the serpent may originally have been a dragon. After the fruit of the tree has been eaten, Genesis III, 14, reads: 'And the Lord God said unto the serpent, Because

Above The course of the moon, like the course of the sun, was sometimes represented as a snake carrying the signs of the zodiac on its back, as shown on this Assyrian boundary stone. This is supported by a thirteenth-century Vatican Codex: 'Then the all-wise Demiurge, by his highest command, set in motion the great dragon with the spangled crown. I mean the twelve signs of the zodiac which are borne on his back.'

Above *A seal of St Servatius in Masstricht Cathedral shows the goddess of fate as a dragon with 7 heads.*

Above *The crucified serpent, from a fourteenth-century Biblia Panperin. Christ was identified with his serpent by the Gnostics.*

thou hast done this, thou art cursed above all cattle, and above every beast of the field; upon thy belly shalt thou go, and dust shalt thou eat all the days of thy life.' A serpent goes upon its belly in any case, which makes that part of the curse rather meaningless. A dragon, however, usually has legs, either two or four, and, deprived of them as a punishment, would become the snake-like creature which appears in pictures of the event. It is true that Genesis speaks specifically of a serpent at that point, but the Bible has passed through various translations before reaching its present form – and in any case, the words 'dragon' and 'serpent' are frequently seen to be interchangeable throughout the Bible, for instance: 'And the great dragon was cast out, that old serpent.' (Revelations XII, 9)

In the usual interpretation of the forbidden tree, that it was the Tree of Knowledge, it seems strange that learned Christians, who included monks, themselves guardians of knowledge, should readily accept that it was wrong of the serpent-dragon to offer the fruit from the tree to early man. The Gnostics, in fact, saw the whole picture quite differently. To put their beliefs briefly and crudely: the gnostics regard the Jewish Yahweh, the architect of this world, as a demi-urge, bad-tempered, vengeful and the father of all evil. In their view, the High God had nothing to do with the creation. (However, they do believe that Jesus, son of the High God, was the salvation of mankind. The demi-urge allowed him to die on the cross in order to conquer him, but by means of the passion, crucifixion and resurrection, Jesus was victorious and mankind saved forever.) In his book *The History of the Devil and the Idea of Evil*, (1900) Dr Paul Carus says:

> One particularly interesting sect of gnostics is called the Ophites, or serpent worshippers. The demi-urge, so they hold, on recognising the danger that might result from the emancipation of men through gnosis (ie: knowledge or enlightenment) forbade him to eat of the fruit of the tree of knowledge. But the God, the highest Lord, the all-good and all-wise deity, took compassion on man and sent the serpent to induce him to eat of the tree of knowledge so that he might escape the bondage of ignorance in which Yahweh, the demi-urge, tried to hold him.

Whatever the true meaning of the story of the Garden of Eden, the theme of man trying to take something precious from a tree or cave guarded by a snake or dragon appears in mythologies from all over the world.

In gnostic representations of the crucifixion, Christ is sometimes represented as a snake in the belief that the being who twice helped mankind took that form, first when he offered him wisdom and second when he offered himself as bait to the demi-urge, to save humanity. In defence of snakes, Christ himself is quoted: 'Be thou therefore wise as serpents, harmless as doves.' (Matthew X, 16) And it is remembered that when Moses raised the brazen serpent in the wilderness it was prophesied that 'even so shall the son of man be lifted up'.

The Gnostics, though, represent a very narrow body of Christianity, and the Bible in general, both Old and New Testaments, regards the serpent, and the dragon he evolved from or became, with revulsion and dread. However, the first actual dragons, the Babylonian dragons of the first creation myths, which myths scholars generally regard as inviting close comparison with much of the Old Testament, were not wholly evil but, as will be seen, were ambivalent both in nature and in impact.

The First Dragons

It has often been suggested, and most often during the late nineteenth century, that the first dragons were the giant reptiles whose fossil remains have been found in most parts of the world, or even that they were animals which are still extant – such as the monitor lizard, the Komodo Dragon.

As 'dragon' comes from the Greek, the word did not exist in pre-Hellenic times which means that the dragons of the earlier mythologies cannot be precisely identified by textual references. They must be identified by their appearance and attributes – the most basic of which are that they are serpentine, reptilian, associated with water and immensely powerful. Legs, wings, ability to change shape and size, fiery breath and a hoard of treasure are secondary attributes which do not always appear.

Like the cosmic serpent, the early dragon plays a vital role in primitive creation myths. Its early association with water caused it to be represented most frequently as the monster of watery chaos, and occasionally slightly less dramatically as weather phenomena involving rains and flooding. Often this creature opposed the creation and had to be vanquished by the god, just as mankind had to vanquish the chaotic and destructive aspects

Right *An Iranian bronze (c1900 BC) of a composite animal with a lion's body, a serpent's head and neck and the claws of a bird of prey: this is the dragon which was featured many centuries later on the Ishtar Gate at Babylon. The bronze is socketed and may originally have been the head of an ornamental staff.*

of nature in order to build. In one particular instance, the actual body of the slain dragon was used as the raw material for building.

Using these guide lines the first dragons of all appear in Sumerian mythology. This is particularly interesting because, as S.G.F. Branden, says in his book *Creation Legends of the Ancient Near East*:

There is general agreement that the foundations of Mesopotamian culture were laid down by the Sumerians. This is particularly to be seen in the matter of religion: the Sumerian pantheon continued to be accepted and venerated by the Babylonians and Assyrians, with their respective local or national deities woven into the system.

And the Mesopotamian culture had a fundamental influence on other cultures in the Near East and, ultimately, elsewhere.

Among the Sumerian myths which were accepted by the Babylonians and Assyrians were stories of battles between a god and a dragon. Although translations and commentaries differ, because the tablets upon which the myths were inscribed are incomplete, damaged and often unclear, one of the earliest of Sumerian myths appears to tell of a combat between Ninurta, a god-hero, and Asag, a monster-dragon. There is also the story of the giant sea-dragon Labbu who was so terrible in aspect that the very gods trembled before him and had to appoint a champion to overcome him. A similar myth tells of the conflict between Ninurta, or in later Assyrian hymns Marduk, and the awesome storm bird, Zu. Zu, who came from Kur, the underworld, stole the tablets of power from Enlil, the high-god, which theft caused Enlil to become so enfeebled that he was unable to take any action. Enlil chose Marduk as his champion, who, after a terrible struggle overcame Zu and recovered the magic tablets.

Below *This reconstruction of the Ishtar Gate, once an entrance to part of the city of Babylon, contains some of the original tiles. The dog-like dragon, similar to those of Iranian mythology of about 2000 BC, is said to be the Musrussu dragon, personal symbol of Marduk, the champion of the gods.*

Kur, the Sumerian word for the underworld, was sometimes also applied to the personification of the underworld, and this leads to a slightly more detailed story, that of the slaying of the monster, Kur, by Ninurta, here described as the son of Enlil. Significantly Kur is referred to as 'the monster who held back the waters' – the creature which also appears in Indian and South American mythologies. When Kur is slain the primal waters are no longer held in check and there are terrible floods. Ninurta solves this problem by piling stones on the dead body of Kur, thus creating a wall against the floods. It is interesting that even as early as this the dragon is seen to be holding something back, guarding a treasure, in this case water, the most valuable commodity available to man. However, the story is incomplete because the tablets on which it is inscribed are badly damaged, and it is never stated why it was felt necessary for Ninurta to destroy Kur. There is no indication that he was withholding water to the extent of causing drought – although this may be thought to be implicit in the story – and his destruction causes a serious problem.

It is considered quite likely that this monster, Kur, at least partly inspired the stories of the legendary Tiamat, the ocean of salt water, who figures in the *Enuma elish*. This is a Babylonian epic poem of about 1,000 lines, recorded on seven clay tablets, which originated as a liturgical chant associated with the Babylonian New Year Festival. These tablets have been almost completely recovered and restored, although there are still gaps and controversially translated words. It was untitled and is known by its opening words – *Enuma elish* – translated as 'When on high . . .'

Enuma elish is a complex and sometimes contradictory epic, probably because various earlier traditions have almost certainly been woven together. It is principally concerned with Marduk. The epic begins:

Above *Early nineteenth-century Japanese ivory netsuke (retaining toggle), one of a series of 12 depicting the creatures of the Chinese zodiac. It is interesting that of all the zodiac animals – rat, ox, tiger, hare, dragon, snake, horse, sheep, monkey, cock, dog and boar – the dragon is the only one whose existence is in doubt. There is a marked similarity between this creature and the one depicted on the bronze below.*

Left *A Sassanian bronze, from the fourth century, found in Afghanistan. It is said to be an invention of Iranian mythology representing Ahriman, the great power of darkness and evil.*

19

Above *A Babylonian boundary stone (c.1120 BC) recording a gift of land to Gula-eres by Eanna-sum-iddiuna, governor of the Sea-land. The gods who are invoked to protect the dead are represented by their carved symbols in relief. Centre left shows the Musrussu dragon. It also shows the world-encircling serpent.*

When on high the heaven had not been named,
Firm ground below had not been called by name,
Nought but primordial Apsu, their begetter,
(And) Mummu-Tiamat, she who bore them all,
Their waters co-mingling as a single body . . . .

From this union are born two pairs of deities, Lahmu and Lahamu and Anshar and Kishar. From the union of Anshar and Kishar is born Anu who was the highest god of the traditional Mesopotamian pantheon. In fact, all gods and heroes were descended from Tiamat and Apsu, so that Marduk was closely related to Tiamat, whom he ultimately had to kill. The offspring of Tiamat and Apsu begin to offend them by behaving in an unseemly fashion, and Apsu decides to destroy them. At this stage Tiamat defends creation, although her attitude changes drastically later on. Enki, the son of Anu, discovers that Apsu is intent on destruction and, by means of magic, first makes Apsu unconscious and then kills him.

Marduk then appears in the story, born of the union of Enki and Damkina, but somehow born fully grown, just as Athene sprang fully grown from the head of Zeus. Now that Apsu has been killed, Tiamat is roused to anger and virtually declares war on creation. To help her, she gives birth to a brood of monsters, including dragons. No one can face Tiamat, much less overcome her, until Marduk is persuaded to become the champion of the gods. By way of premature reward, or perhaps as a pre-condition, the other gods make him supreme. The epic says: 'We have granted the kingship over the universe entire.'

The actual conflict is described quite briefly. Tiamat opens her mouth to destroy Marduk by swallowing him and he causes a wind to enter into her body and distend her so that she cannot close it again. He then fires an arrow through her open mouth and straight into her heart. This method of dragon-slaying is not unlike much later representations – for instance, those which show St George dispatching a dragon by inserting a lance down its throat. There may be an iconographic connection here, or it may simply be that the only possible way to kill a monster is to strike at its one vulnerable place. When Marduk has killed Tiamat the epic goes on to say:

He split her like a shellfish in two parts,
Half of her he set up and sealed it as the sky,
Pulled down the bar and posted guards.
He bade them to allow not her waters to escape.

It seems that Tiamat herself has now become the 'monster that holds back the waters', and it is perhaps worth remembering here that at this period of time it was believed that the earth was entirely surrounded by water and that the fabric of the sky was such that it held these waters back and allowed just sufficient to seep through in the form of rain. This belief is shown clearly on an early Babylonian clay map held in the British Museum.

The epic is quite difficult to understand for various reasons, not least because the universe already exists, although nameless, when Marduk forms half of Tiamat into the sky, and so therefore presumably there already was a sky. Also, nothing is said directly about what happens to the other half of her body, or whether that becomes the earth.

Although there is no doubt that Tiamat spawned dragons, and that dragons feature in the story, there is controversy about whether or not Tiamat was herself a dragon. Alexander Heidel, in his book *The Babylonian Genesis*, says:

> Tiamat is almost universally held to have been a dragon or some serpentine monster of a forbidding aspect .... It has been urged that since *Enuma elish* represents Tiamat as having borne monster serpents, Tiamat herself must have been a great and powerful serpent or serpent-like monster. Against this, however, it must be remembered that Tiamat gave birth also to the good and benevolent gods, who expressly call her 'our bearer', and that, even after she had brought forth monsters, Marduk still refers to her as a woman .... Tiamat was a goddess and as such she could give birth to dragons without herself being a dragon.

Later he comments that it has also been suggested that she must have been a dragon because when Marduk approached her in mortal combat she opened wide her mouth and attempted to swallow him, but points out that Kronos, one of the Titans of mythology, swallowed his children, because he had been told that he, like his father, would be deposed by his own son, and was never considered to be a dragon because of it. However, both dragons and gods are notorious for their shape-changing abilities – Zeus became a swan to seduce Leda, possibly Tiamat became a dragon to face Marduk. Certainly Marduk's symbol is acknowledged to be a dragon, the implication being that Marduk has overcome a dragon which consequently lies submissively at his side or upon his standard.

The pictorial representations which are supposedly of Tiamat mostly appear on Babylonian cylinder seals. These are small cylindrical seals which were rolled across the surface to be impressed rather than being stamped upon it. The earlier ones were the personal seals of individuals, some of the later ones were the official seals of the Assyrian kings and of

Below *This impression from a Babylonian cylinder seal is said to depict Tiamat as a dragon, pursued by a god armed with a thunderbolt who is possibly Marduk. The mingling of Tiamat (the tumultuous sea) and Apsu (the primordial ocean) initiated the creation of the world. Tiamat represents the feminine element which gave birth to the world, and later, in her fury, to a brood of dragons. She symbolizes the blind forces of primitive chaos against which the intelligent gods struggle. The legend is told in the Babylonian epic,* Enuma elish.

temples. They depict many stories other than that of Tiamat, and are one of the principal sources of information on the period because they survived; being small and made of stone they did not break, and also it is believed that they were collected as family heirlooms and thus preserved more carefully than they might otherwise have been.

The cylinder seal most often associated with Tiamat shows a horned and serpentine dragon with two short arms, being pursued by a god armed with thunderbolts, but the name of Tiamat is nowhere found in connection with this seal. It is even possible that the dragon depicted is Kur. Nevertheless, Tiamat was the mother of dragons, and Alexander Heidel says: 'In general, it should be remembered that dragons were most likely much more numerous in Babylonian and Assyrian religious belief than the available cuneiform records would indicate.' It must always be remembered that material from this period is extremely fragmentary and that iconographic representations, when divorced from text, are open to misinterpretation. So Kur is probably the first dragon, followed by the brood of Tiamat. The first St George, or at least the first human, as opposed to divine, dragon-slayer, may well have been the hero of *The Epic of Gilgamesh*, or so it is suggested by Noah Kramer, Professor of Assyriology, in his book *From the Tablets of Sumer*. *The Epic of Gilgamesh* is a story of the third millenium BC, originally inscribed on clay tablets, and now available in paperback! Excavations of clay tablets have indicated that the story was studied and translated in ancient times all over the Near East. Professor Kramer says:

> Orientalists first came to know of him (Gilgamesh) and his heroic exploits not from Sumerian but from Semitic sources. He is the protagonist in the Babylonian epic now generally admitted to be the most significant literary creation of the whole of ancient Mesopotamia.

The epic is the continuing story of the exploits of the hero Gilgamesh, only one of which is the slaying of the dragon, Humbaba, who prowls in a cedar forest, the wood from which Gilgamesh and his people need for building. Humbaba, who is sometimes described as a man, a giant, has been appointed guardian of the forest by Enlil, father of the gods. Of him it is said: 'When he roars it is like the torrent of the storm, his breath is like fire, and his jaws are death itself.' He is not specifically described as a dragon, but has the attributes of one, including the shape-changing ability common to so many later dragons. He is overcome with the help of the god Shamash and, once it is clear that he is in the power of Gilgamesh, he begs for mercy, offering to become the servant of the hero. But mercy is not granted, he is killed with three sword blows to the throat – a bad decision as it turns out, since his death offends those gods who support him. There may be an echo of this potential subjugation of the dragon in representations of St George or St Martha leading a dragon with a girdle prior to dispatching him in front of the assembled people.

This kind of hero versus monster conflict, which appears in so many subsequent dragon myths of all cultures, is clearly derived from the god versus primeval-dragon conflict of the creation myths, and also of myths which describe vital confrontations which took place after the creation was complete. This confrontation is frequently between a monster and a

Below *The most famous Assyro-Babylonian hero Gilgamesh is seen here on a bas-relief from Khorsabad (eighth century BC) holding a lion.*

storm-god who is armed with thunderbolts or lightning shafts. Indra appears armed in this way, as do the Sumerian gods and the rain-god of the Mayas. This battle of the storm-god with watery chaos itself may be echoed in later Semitic myth where the spirit of God is said to move upon the face of the waters.

It is possible that the Sumerian dragon myth reached Egypt towards the end of the third millenium BC and inspired the legend of the huge sea-serpent Apophis (or Apep or Apop), enemy of the sun god, Re. Many texts contain references to the conquest of Apophis, and in one of these Seth is shown to be the agent of victory, rather as Marduk is the champion of the gods when all are threatened by Tiamat. S.H. Hooke says in *Middle Eastern Mythology*:

> Another text containing a curse against the enemies of the Pharoah says 'They (ie: the king's enemies) shall be like the snake Apophis on New Year's morning'. Here the snake symbolises the darkness which the sun defeats every morning as he begins his journey in his heavenly barque through the heavens, and especially on New Year's Morning. We have here an interesting parallel with the victory of Marduk over the dragon Tiamat at the Babylonian New Year Festival.

Commentaries on Egyptian mythology sometimes identify Seth (or Set), the 'formless being' who is the brother and enemy of the vegetation god, Osiris, with a dragon. The mythology of the Hittites, a peoples who settled in Asia Minor at the start of the second millenium, and whose

Above *This papyrus (c.1300 BC) of Hunefer from the Theban Book of the Dead shows the Cat of Re cutting up the demon of darkness, Apophis. Every morning and evening the sun-god succeeded in circumventing his enemy's manoeuvres, and the equilibrium in the universe was achieved as a result of the perpetual struggle between these two powers, which opposed and complemented one another.*

Above The god Ninurta, armed with a thunderbolt, drives a demon resembling a dragon out of his temple. This Assyrian sculpture (c.880 BC), from the Temple of Ninurta at Nimrud, has often been mistaken for a representation of the fight between Tiamat and Marduk.

religion was strongly influenced by that of Babylon, tells of the battle between the storm-god and the dragon Illuyankas. In this myth the dragon initially overcomes the god and only later does the god avenge himself upon the dragon. S.H. Hooke says:

> The later version of the myth has some features which are not found in the earlier version. When the dragon defeated the storm-god he took away his heart and his eyes, a detail which has an echo in the Egyptian myth of the fight between Horus (the son of Osiris) and Seth in which Horus lost one of his eyes.

This facility of the dragon for being identified with opposing sides is one of his most confusing attributes. He can be identified, it seems, with Apophis and also with Seth who overcame Apophis. The dragon will not be pinpointed in any of its manifestations, but to begin to understand some of the shape-shifting it helps to remember two things. One is that, traditionally, the dragon-slayer took on some of the qualities of the slain dragon, and the other is that the dragon is associated with water.

It seems almost reasonable to say that in the beginning there was the dragon. One of the few constants is the association with water, and even that is glossed over in some of the later Western myths. And yet, despite his mutability, it becomes steadily easier to differentiate between a dragon and other mythical beasts once he has established himself.

Classical Dragons

One of the best known and most powerful dragonish creations of classical mythology is Typhon, avenger of the Titans. It is told that the Titans, early nature gods of obscure origin, rebelled against Zeus and the gods of Olympus, just as dark and violent chaos has pitted itself against the powers of heaven and light in so many other early myths. The theme of this battle of the gods and Titans inspired much later art and literature, and Ovid, Spenser, Milton, Rubens, Blake, Keats and Braque each dealt with the drama in a different way.

The Titans were huge and terrible, with serpents' tails for feet, but when they were overthrown the monster sent to avenge them was even more terrible than they had been themselves. Typhon was born of Ge, the Earth, her youngest offspring, and was the largest monster ever to exist. His head reached the stars, his wings blocked the light of the sun, his arms stretched a hundred leagues in each direction and ended in clusters of serpent heads, and from the thighs downwards he was formed entirely of writhing serpents. His roaring and whistling was like that of the most terrible of storm-winds, and from his mouth flew flaming rocks. The full terror of Typhon is captured in Hesiod's *Theogony*, here translated by R. Lattimore, which teaches the origin of the universe.

Left *After Zeus defeated the Titans, he had to fight the Giants. These sons of Earth had legs like serpents, and their feet were formed of reptiles' heads. The Giants were protected by magic devices, and could only be killed by the blows of a mortal and a god both delivered at the same time. Zeus instructed the Sun, Moon, and Dawn to give no light until he could find a magic to make the Giants vulnerable to mortal blows.*

Up from his shoulders
　　there grew a hundred snakes heads,
those of a dreaded dragon,
　　and the heads licked with dark tongues
and from the eyes on
　　the inhuman heads fire glittered
from under the eyelids.
　　From all his heads fire flared
from his eyes' glancing;
　　and inside each one of these horrible heads
there were voices
　　that threw out every sort of horrible sound.

Not surprisingly, the gods of Olympus fled in horror from this awful dragon, and made their way to Egypt. (The story may well contain some historical truth – the description of Typhon is clearly a description of a volcanic eruption. Zeus, who fled initially, turned at last to fight.

Seizing
his weapons, thunder, lightning,
　　and the glowering thunderbolt,
he made a leap from Olympus, and struck,
　　setting fire
to all those wonderful heads set about
　　on the dreaded monster.
Then, when Zeus had put him down
　　with his strokes, Typhoeus
crashed – crippled – and the gigantic earth
　　groaned beneath him,
and the flame from the great lord
　　so thunder-smitten ran out
along the darkening and steep forests
　　of the mountains
as he was struck, and a great part
　　of the earth burned
in the wonderful wind of his heat,
　　and melted . . . in the flash
of the blazing fire.

Zeus buried the conquered Typhon under Mount Etna, where he continues to emit the odd belch from his tomb.

In Greek tradition, this conflict between Zeus and Typhon is sometimes mingled and confused with the conflict between Apollo and Python at Delphi. Delphi was the site of the Delphic Oracle, which Apollo made his own, and there are various interpretations of the slaying by Apollo of whatever creature he found there. According to the Homeric Hymn, when Apollo was in the process of establishing his shrine he discovered a great female serpent (sometimes called Typhaeon and sometimes Delphyne by later writers) which was devastating the land. He fought and killed her and left her body to rot by the shrine – thereafter the place was called Pytho, which in Greek means 'corruption'.

Ovid's version, which was taken from Simonides and Apollodorus, is that when Apollo came to Delphi there was already a shrine there, the shrine of the earth goddess, guarded by Python, who barred his way. Apollo killed Python and took over the shrine.

Euripedes told another version still, which was that when Apollo's mother, Leto, had given birth to him on Delos, she carried him to Delphi where she was attacked by the dragon Python. The baby god saved himself and his mother by sitting up in her arms and shooting arrows at Python. In some of the pictorial representations of this, Apollo's sister, Artemis, is also present, as another child in Leto's arms.

Lucan, Hyginus and others tell that Apollo and his sister, Artemis, were the children of Leto by her affair with the ever-amorous Zeus and that Hera, wife of Zeus, was so jealous of Leto that she sent the serpent Python to chase her from place to place so that she should not be allowed to rest and deliver herself of her children. Nevertheless, she did manage to give birth successfully to both children and, as soon as he was grown, which, as he was a god, was in a matter of months, Apollo pursued Python to Delphi where he killed him.

Left *In Greek mythology, Apollo was the god of light, and the archer god. This print shows him, aged four days, firing an arrow down the throat of Python, a method echoed in Western mythology.*

A somewhat less romantic account, given by Ephorus and Pausanius, is that a brigand called either Python or Drakon was active around Delphi and that the local people asked for Apollo's help, whereupon the god killed the brigand and freed them from his influence.

Whatever the original meaning of the myth, and however much the story may have become confused as various versions and translations were blended together, it seems quite reasonable to accept that Apollo took into his service the oracular serpent of Delphi. There were several of these serpents, called 'dragon' in Greek, who were protected as sacred in both Greek and Roman temples, many of whom were believed to speak as oracles through the mouths of their priestesses. While the primitive Typhon was a dragon of darkness and destruction, here the later serpent-dragon has acquired his association with knowledge and wisdom.

One who consulted the Pythian Oracle at Delphi was the hero Heracles, (or Hercules) who sought the secret of immortality. The oracle advised him to bind himself to the service of Eurystheus for 12 years, and it was upon the orders of this king that Heracles undertook the 12 immense tasks which eventually won him his place among the stars. These 12 labours of Heracles brought him into confrontation with a range of creatures, all of them greater, and stronger, and swifter than any earthly counterpart. And among them were two dragons – the seven-headed Hydra, and Ladon the dragon who guarded the Golden Apples of the Hesperides, the daughters of the evening.

The destruction of the Hydra of Lerna was the second labour assigned to Heracles – the first being the slaying of the Nemean Lion, whose skin the hero is seen to wear in so many of the pictorial representations of his exploits. It is told that the Hydra was a seven-headed (though some say 50, or 100, or 1,000-headed) snake which lived beneath a plane tree at the source of the River Amymone and haunted the nearby Lernaen swamp, terrorizing the area, as is the wont of dragons. Supposedly it was a water-serpent, born of Typhon and Echidne. Echidne was part beautiful woman and part snake and her grisly progeny included Cerberus, the three-headed Hound of Hell, the Chimaera with its lion's head and dragon's tail, and even the Sphinx and the Nemean Lion itself. The Hydra was not only malicious and venomous; each time one of its heads was severed more grew in its place. Heracles used fire to solve this problem, applying a burning brand to the stump of each neck after he had severed the head, so that no more could grow, and in this way completed the labour. He dipped his arrows in the venom of the dead dragon and thereafter they were deadly poisonous.

One explanation of this story has been that the Hydra was, indeed, an exceptionally venomous water snake, and that the many heads either symbolized the speed with which a snake can whip its head from side to side, or else were a later addition to make the story, when retold, more dramatic. Another possibility, borne out by the fact that the monster lived at the source of a river and near a swamp, is that the Hydra was a system of underground rivers and tributaries which habitually broke out and inundated the surrounding lands; stop up one outlet and the water would find several more. In this case, Heracles' method was first to dry out the land by fire and then systematically to seal off the outlets.

A similar explanation has been put forward for the dragon Ladon, who guarded the tree of Golden Apples given to Hera, as a wedding gift, by

Below *Eursytheus, ruler of Greece, commanded Heracles to bring him the Golden Apples of the Hesperides. To get to the apples, Heracles had to kill the dragon Ladon who guarded them. This image is similar to those of the dragon guarding the Trees of Life and Knowledge, and ties in with later ideas of the dragon guarding a treasure. (engraving by François Verdier)*

Left *The Hydra of Lerna had many heads, and its breath was so poisonous that whoever felt it died. Heracles, here wearing the skin of the Nemean lion, tried to kill it by cutting off the heads, but when he severed a head, two more grew in its place. So he set the neighbouring forest on fire, and with redhot brands burnt the serpents' heads. He then soaked his arrows in the Hydra's blood which made them deadly poisonous. (engraving by Christofan Robotta)*

Mother Earth. Some say that Ladon, too, was a child of Typhon and Echidne, others that he was borne of Mother Earth and of no father, as Typhon himself was. Hera entrusted her tree to the three Hesperides, and the garden where it grew was known as the Garden of the Hesperides. There are disputes about where the garden was located, but it seems possible that it was in a fertile part of present-day Libya. The stories say that Hera discovered that the Hesperides were pilfering her apples and that she instructed the dragon, Ladon, to coil himself round the tree and guard it.

In order to accomplish his set task of taking a few of these apples of immortality back to King Eurystheus, Heracles had to slay the dragon, and in memory of this feat his shield ever afterwards bore the likeness of a dragon, which Homer described in heraldic terms as 'The scaly horror of a dragon, coiled full in the central field, unspeakable, with eyes oblique, retorted, that askant shot gleaming fire'.

The proffered explanations diminish the drama of the story, as explanations so often do. One was that there were never any apples but that the Hesperides owned a flock of golden-coloured sheep who were guarded by a shepherd called Draco and that, in order to steal the sheep, Heracles had first to murder or abduct this Draco. Another is that whatever it was that was of value in the garden, the garden itself was almost inaccessible, on a promontory, at the edge of which there was a waterfall which resembled a fall of snakes guarding the land behind, a fall which Heracles would have to conquer to gain access.

While these, and other, explanations must always have been available, they never caught the popular imagination, and a far more satisfactory image is that of the ever-watchful dragon, guarding the Tree of the Golden Apples as he guarded the Trees of Life and Knowledge. An early version of a dragon with a hoard, although in this case he was appointed guardian and can be seen as faithful servant rather than as the greedy protector of his own personal treasure that he was later thought to be.

Another who consulted the Delphic Oracle was King Cadmus, the founder of the city of Thebes. Cadmus was one of the brothers of Europa. When Europa was abducted by Zeus, in the form of a bull, her father ordered his sons to search for her, and not to return until they had found her. Because they had no idea where she might have been taken, they all set off in different directions.

Cadmus and his companions searched fruitlessly until, at last, reaching Delphi, they enquired of the Oracle where Europa might be. The Pythoness instructed Cadmus to abandon the search, to buy a cow and drive her, and to found a city wherever the cow finally rested. This he did, and the cow chose to rest where the city of Thebes eventually stood.

Cadmus knew that the cow must be sacrificed to Athene and he sent some of his companions to fetch water for the cleansing before the sacrifice, from the nearby Spring of Ares (or Mars). What he did not realize was that this spring was guarded by a terrible dragon, traditionally the guardian of springs, lakes and wells in both Eastern and Western

Below Many classical mythological creatures had dragon-like attributes. Triton, Poseidon's son, had a scaled body, and lived in the sea. He could raise or quieten the waves, and had the duo-nature common in dragons. Here, Heracles fights the Triton.

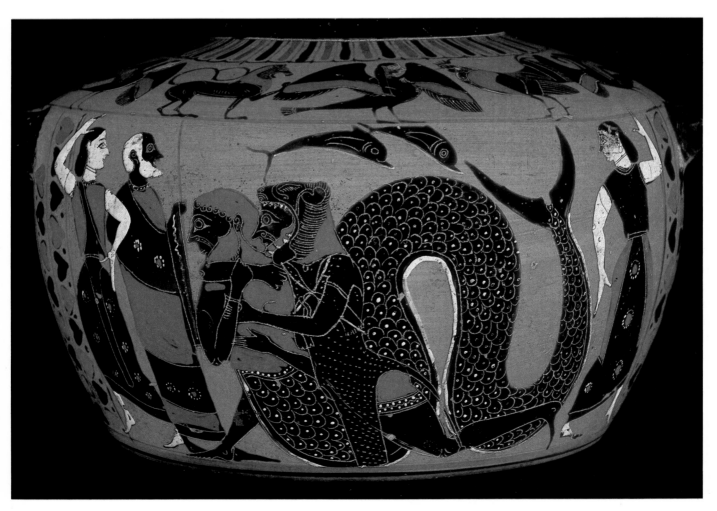

mythology. This spirit of the spring killed most of Cadmus' companions and when he went in search of them and saw what had happened, he himself attacked it, crushing its head with a rock. Ovid describes the first sight of the dragon (*Metamorphoses*; Book III, 35, translated by H. J. Riley):

> Hidden in this cave dwelt the serpent of Mars, a creature with a wonderful golden crest; fire flashed from its eyes, its body was all puffed up with poison, and from its mouth, set with a triple row of teeth, flickered a three-forked tongue . . . . It was as huge as the serpent that twines between the two Bears in the sky, if its full length were seen uncoiled.

It is interesting that Ovid describes all his dragons, and there are several in the *Metamorphoses*, as wearing crests on their heads. Ovid was a poet and story teller who lived from 43 BC to AD 17, and his dragons are presented as fictitious. Nevertheless, he took his themes and conventions from Greek mythology and presumably the convention of the crest came with the rest.

Cadmus then made the sacrifice to Athene, who appeared to him and ordered him to sow the dragon's teeth, like seeds. This he did, and instantly armed warriors grew up, complete, from the earth, and began to fight amongst themselves. At last only five, the ancestors of the Thebans, remained. These five pledged themselves to the service of Cadmus, but first Cadmus himself was bonded for a year to the service of Ares, as a penance for having killed his guardian dragon.

Not all of the dragon's teeth were sown by Cadmus. A few were retained by Athene, and these figured in the story of Jason and his quest for the Golden Fleece. There are various suggestions about what this fleece may actually have been. One is that it was the skin of a magical flying ram, on the back of which Phrixus and Helle escaped from their murderous father and stepmother. Helle fell off and drowned in the water later named in her honour, the Hellespont, but Phrixus was borne safely to Colchis where he sacrificed the ram to Zeus in gratitude and gave its fleece into the keeping of the King of Colchis, Aeëtes. Aeëtes believed that his fortunes were bound up with the fleece and protected it as he would protect his kingdom. It was guarded, just as the Golden Apples of the Hesperides were guarded, by a terrible and unsleeping dragon.

Other explanations say that Jason and the Argonauts were actually in search of gold, which was panned in the rivers of Colchis and stored in bags of sheepskin. Yet others that it was not gold but amber, or even that it was an alchemical work, written on vellum or sheepskin, and describing how to transmute base metal into gold. Whatever it was, Jason was sent in search of it by King Pelias, who had been warned by an oracle that he must beware of a man wearing only one sandal, and Jason had just lost a sandal when he first met Pelias. Sending him to fetch the fleece was tantamount to sending him to his death, but the gods were on his side and he prevailed.

King Aeëtes promised to give Jason the fleece if he could perform certain seemingly impossible tasks. However, Eros, the god of love, caused Aeëtes' daughter, the enchantress Medea, to fall in love with Jason, and with her on his side the tasks became possible. He was ordered to yoke two magical, fire-breathing oxen, use them to plough an enormous field, and then sow the dragon's teeth given to him by Athene.

Above *Cadmus slaying the serpent of Mars, referred to as a dragon in so many versions of the story. Towards the end of his life, Cadmus and his wife, Harmonia, reigned over Illyria. They were changed into dragons and transported to the Island of the Blessed.*

With Medea's help he managed the first two tasks, and then sowed the teeth. Up sprang the armed warriors, who, it seemed, would destroy him. But he managed to provoke them to fight amongst themselves, just as the warriors who grew from the first batch of teeth had done, so that he only had to dispatch the wounded survivors.

But the King did not keep to his part of the bargain, and refused to part with the Golden Fleece, and so Jason was forced to steal it from under the eye of the huge and immortal 'dragon of a thousand coils'. According to Apollonius of Rhodes, in his poem *Argonautica*, Medea used spells and herbs to lull the great dragon to sleep and Jason stole the fleece without harming or disturbing its guardian. An alternative version, borne out by a decoration on an Etruscan cup, is that the dragon who guarded the fleece was a sea monster, with whom Jason fought. In the course of their battle the monster swallowed the hero and was only forced to disgorge him, half dead, by the intercession of Athene. The Etruscan artwork shows the fleece quite clearly, dangling from a tree behind the dragon.

So a dragon of chaos, dragons of wisdom and guardian dragons all featured in classical mythology – and a forerunner of St George was there, too. Gilgamesh may have been the 'first St George', but the first classical St George was neither Heracles nor Jason, but Perseus. The story of Perseus and Andromeda has all the elements of the well-known romance of St George and the Dragon, and most authorities believe it to have been the basis of the Georgian legend. The principal difference seems to have been that Perseus was offered a kingdom and the rescued girl's hand in

Right *The story of the quest for the Golden Fleece has many variations. This Attic vase shows the dragon spewing forth Jason after it drank the potion prepared by Athene. The fleece hangs on a tree in the background and the picture presents a similar image to Jonah and the whale. The allegory of the hero being swallowed by the dragon is common. The Bible tells how Nebuchadnezzar 'hath devoured me, he hath crushed me, he hath made me an empty vessel, he hath swallowed me up like a dragon, he hath filled his belly with my delicates, he hath cast me out'.* (Jeremiah 51:34)

marriage by way of reward. There was none of the altruism of the earlier heroes whose chief concern was to save the world from chaos, nor of the later saints who sought to inspire it to Christianity.

The most common version of the story is that as Perseus returned from his task of cutting off the head of the Gorgon, Medusa, flying by means of the winged sandals lent to him by the Stygian nymphs, he saw a beautiful naked girl chained to a rock at the edge of a cliff, her feet already washed by the incoming sea. At the top of the cliff stood two people, a man and a woman, watching in obvious distress, and he went to them to ask what was happening. He learned that the girl was Andromeda and the couple were her parents, King Cepheus and Queen Cassiopeia. The Queen had rashly boasted that both she and her daughter were more beautiful than the sea nymphs, the Nereids. The nymphs had heard her and had complained to Poseidon (or Neptune), King of the Seas, that they had been insulted. Poseidon sent a flood and a sea monster to devastate the land, and the King hurriedly consulted an oracle to learn how this inundation could be averted. He was told that the only way to placate the sea nymphs was to offer Andromeda, his only daughter, to the sea monster, and accordingly she was chained to the rock to await its arrival.

Perseus offered to slay the monster and free the Princess, and her parents offered him marriage with their daughter and a kingdom if he should succeed. The dragon rose in a storm from out of the seas, jaws agape to swallow its prey, and Perseus flew over it and took it by surprise from above, some say killing it with three stab wounds to the heart, others say decapitating it with a stroke. Although there were further complications in that it turned out that Andromeda, although willing to marry Perseus, was already promised to someone else, the wedding did take place and the ending was a happy one.

The mythographers were not the only classical writers to talk of dragons and when, for instance, the historian Pliny (AD 23–79) writes of them his intention is clearly to write of a reality and not of a fiction. In Book VIII of his *Histories* he says: 'India bringeth forth the biggest elephants, and also the dragons, that are continually at variance with them, and evermore fighting, and those of such greatnesse that they can easily clasp and wind them around the elephants, and withall tie them fast with a knot.' According to Pliny, this recurring battle between elephant and dragon usually ended in deadlock, literally. The dragon would wind himself around the body of the elephant and impart a fatal sting, the elephant would then fall and in its death throes crush the dragon under its weight.

The classical dragon was powerful, colourful, and an important element in many stories but it was in the East that his power was strongest and where he was revered and venerated the most.

Above *According to the bestiaries (including this illustration from an early sixteenth-century English bestiary), the panther considers only the dragon as its enemy. After it has dined, the panther sleeps for three days, and on awakening, belches, and all the animals hear this and follow its sweet breath. The dragon, however, hides in fear, and unable to bear the smell becomes torpid and half dead. The panther symbolizes Christ, the dragon the devil.*

Below *A ninth-century drawing of Jonah in the belly of the whale, here looking more like a dragon. It is said that a pearl was suspended inside the belly of the creature which gave light to Jonah. In China, the pearl was often a lunar image, the spiritual essence of the universe. A dragon swallowing the pearl was said to have caused the waning of the moon, and belching it forth, the waxing. (Khludor Psalter, Monastery of St Nicholas, Preobrazhenska, USSR)*

Eastern Dragons

Above *According to the eleventh-century Persian* Book of Kings, *Gushtasp, a prince, marries a daughter of Caesar, and on behalf of a suitor of another of Caesar's daughters, kills the dragon that has been destroying the countryside. Gushtasp, like Western dragon-slayers, becomes a hero, though he is unusual in the interpretation of the Eastern dragon.*

Right *A Persian illumination showing the biblical story of Moses and his brother Aaron exorcizing the dragon as told in* Numbers *ch. 21. The people of Israel complain that they have been led into the wilderness where there is no food and water. The Lord sends a plague of fiery serpents which bite the people, who turn to Moses and repent. God tells Moses to make a fiery serpent and to set it on a brass pole, when this is done everyone will be healed.*

The dragons of China and Japan are almost exclusively benevolent. This separates them from the Western dragons, and even from the Sumerian and Persian dragons, to such an extent that it may be more reasonable to consider them as different creatures, rather than as the same creature interpreted differently.

In his book *The Awakening of Japan* (1904), the Japanese author Okakura says:

> The Eastern dragon is not the gruesome monster of medieval imagination but the genius of strength and goodness. He is the spirit of change, and therefore of life itself .... Hidden in the caverns of inaccessible mountains, or coiled in the unfathomed depths of the sea, he awaits the time when he slowly rouses himself into activity. He unfolds himself in the storm clouds; washes his mane in the blackness of the seething whirlpools. His claws are in the fork of the lightning, his scales begin to glisten in the bark of rain-swept pine trees. His voice is heard in the hurricane, which, scattering the withered leaves of the forest, quickens a new spring.

And that is quite a precise definition of the Eastern dragon, Chinese as well as Japanese. But there is more precision yet, especially in the case of the specifically Chinese dragon, whose appearance, several types and modes of behaviour are all catalogued in detail.

In *Legend in Japanese Art*, L. Joly gives the accepted description of the dragon:

> The Chinese call the dragon 'lung' because it is deaf. It is the largest of scaly animals, and it has nine characteristics. Its head is like a camel's, its horns like a deer's, its eyes like a hare's, its ears like a bull's, its neck like an iguana's, its belly like a frog's, its scales like those of a carp, its paws like a tiger's, and its claws like an eagle's. It has nine times nine scales, it being the extreme of a lucky number. On each side of its mouth are whiskers, under its chin a bright pearl, on the top of its head the 'poh shan' or foot-rule, without which it cannot ascend to heaven. The scales of its throat are reversed. Its breath changes into clouds from which come either fire or rain. The dragon is fond of the flesh of sparrows and swallows, it dreads the centipede and silk dyed of five colours. It is also afraid of iron.

In *The Dragon in China and Japan* (1858), Dr M.W. de Visser says: 'The *Pen ts'ao kang-muh*, the famous standard work on Natural History and Materia Medica, written in the latter half of the fifteenth century by Li Shi

كفت قوله تعالى قلنا لا تخف انك انت الاعلى فرمان آمد كه يا موسى مترس كه دست تو بر
دست ايشان باشد هر كجا حق آمد باطل وابو و جاء الحق وزهق الباطل ندا آمد كه بيفكن آنچه

در دست داری موسى عصا بيفكند بر زمين در دست كرد بدان ميدان برآمد اژدهائى عظيم كشت و دم حلقه كرد

Above *A seal from the Hardinge Collection with the benevolent dragon of the East holding a pearl under its chin. Like the dragon itself, the pearl does not always hold the same imagery and has been called the symbol of thunder, of the moon, of the sun, of the egg emblem, of the dual influence of nature, and the pearl of potentiality.*

Chen, says, "The dragon's nature is rough and fierce, and yet he likes beautiful gems and . . . is fond of (roasted) swallows. He is afraid of iron, of the *wang* plant (a kind of grain plant similar to 'swallow oats'), of centipedes, of the leaves of the *lien* tree (*Melia azedarach*), and of five-coloured silk thread".' And the Sinologist Dr S. Wells Williams says: 'Its voice is like the jingling of copper pans.'

It is possible that there may be a connection between the dragon's love of eating swallows or sparrows and the habits of crocodiles, who lie basking with jaws agape and allow birds to move in and out of their mouths, picking their teeth. The dragon's fear of iron is as well documented as his love of swallows, and it is said that he can be killed only by a single needle of iron which conjures up a mental picture of the conquering hero's lance.

Dragons were believed to lay eggs, and the young dragon to remain in its egg for 3,000 years – 1,000 in the water, 1,000 in the mountains, and 1,000 in the land of men. These eggs may occasionally have been snakes' eggs, but more often they were beautiful stones of five colours, which gave off water, or at least moisture, when rain was about. It was unwise to be in possession of one at the moment of birth for it would hatch in the form of a tiny worm or snake and grow within minutes into a full-sized dragon which would whirl up to the sky in a thunderstorm, tearing its way out through the roof. Whirlwinds and waterspouts are thus explained as a young dragon ascending to heaven. Empty dragon eggs are said to be preserved in some monasteries, each taking the form of an exceptionally beautiful stone with a small hole in it, and one monastery preserved a dragon egg which had died, that is, stopped giving off moisture. The foetus was said to be visible inside. Dragon eggs, incidentally, should not be confused with 'thunder stones' which are prehistoric stone weapons once considered by the Chinese, and by the Japanese, to be thunderbolts.

The Eastern dragons were assuredly weather-lords. Floods were caused by dragons fighting in the water and storms by dragons fighting in the air. Lightning was heavenly fire sent to stop the dragon fights, for dragons fear fire. This last might be considered odd, in view of the dragon's own fiery breath, but the Chinese writer Wang Fu said: 'Dragon fire and human fire are opposite. If dragon fire comes into contact with wetness it flames, and if it meets water it burns. If one drives it away by means of fire, it stops burning and its flames are extinguished.'

The Chinese classics teach that the dragon is thunder and also that he is a creature of the waters who rests in pools in the winter and rises in the form of rain clouds in spring. In the autumn, the dry season, he sinks back into the pools where he sleeps as he waits for the spring. De Visser says: '. . . the whirlwinds . . . which form water spouts and carry heavy objects into the air, were looked upon as dragons winding their way to the sky amidst thunder and rain. Holes in the ground, due to volcanic eruptions and emitting smoke, were thought to be the spots from where dragons which had been lying in the earth had dashed forth and flown to heaven.'

Always it is made clear that the dragon must fly up to the sky before the rain can fall to earth and so, in times of drought, various methods were employed to persuade, or even to frighten, the dragon into leaving his pool and rising in the form of a cloud. Sometimes gongs were beaten, so that the dragon, although deaf, would respond to their vibration. Sometimes a rod of iron was used to stir up a dragon pond, and, although there is no traceable connection, there is something strangely reminiscent of this in the Uccello painting where St George pierces the dragon with a lance and a whirling rain cloud obligingly gathers in the sky. At the water festival on the fifth day of the fifth month, dragon boat races were deliberately organized in such a way that they seemed to represent fighting dragons in the hope that this would precipitate a real dragon fight with its accompanying heavy rains. And sometimes it was possible to make the dragon rise by frightening him with effigies of the Garuda, or wonderful bird, who was the deadly enemy of the Nagas in Hindu mythology.

The pearl under the dragon's chin is a subject of great controversy, especially when it appears not under the chin at all but spinning in the air, pursued by one or two dragons. There are a number of conflicting interpretations of the identity and symbolism of this 'sacred pearl'. Like the dragon itself, the image may not always carry the same meaning. Pearl symbolism, like lunar symbolism with which it is connected, is extremely complex but, in a necessary over-simplification, the pearl can be said to stand most often for 'truth' and 'life' − perhaps even the everlasting life which is made available to those who perceive the truth and attain enlightenment. In connection with the dragon the pearl has been called the image of thunder, of the moon, of the sun, of the egg emblem of the dual influences of nature, and the 'pearl of potentiality'. Each interpretation seems as acceptable as the next, the only really unsatisfactory one being that the pearl is a spider, metamorphosed into a ball, because legend says that dragons have an especial fondness for teasing spiders!

The pearl is depicted as a spiral or a globe; it is sometimes red, sometimes gold, sometimes the bluish white of a true pearl; it is often accompanied by little jagged flashes that seem to spark out from it, like flames; and it almost always has an appendage in the form of a small undulating sprout, not unlike the first young shoot from a bean.

At first glance it seems most likely that the pearl is indeed the image of thunder rolling. Dragons are weather-lords and storms are caused by dragon fights in the sky, and so it seems probable that a storm would be depicted as two dragons fighting over the thunder itself. What is more, the spiral is traditionally the symbol of thunder, and some of the spiral pearls emit flashes of what could be red and gold lightning. Some authorities have suggested that the pearl is a thunderball belched forth by the dragons, but, although this may be true, it doesn't ring true to the average observer. The dragons seem so obviously to be in attitudes of pursuit, reaching out eagerly to clutch at the elusive object, mouths open in anticipation and eyes bulging with greed. Or at least that is one way of looking at them. Look at the same picture in a different mood and the dragons, or dragon if there is only one, are obviously playing ball with the object, rolling it around the heavens and tossing it to and fro with a kind of gleeful abandon.

But in other pictures, in which the pearl does indeed look like a pearl, pale and translucent, and in which the flashes of red-gold 'lightning' are missing, it is far easier to see it as the moon which is, after all, the most pearl-like thing in the sky. The moon, pearls, dragons and snakes are inextricably linked. Like the snake which is reborn when it sheds its skin, the moon is reborn each month, and both are symbols of immortality. Like the dragon, the moon is always associated with water; its undeniable power over the tides is believed to extend to all liquids on earth. And at one time it was believed that pearls were dropped from the moon into the sea, where they were swallowed by oysters. The dragons who lived in the sea were said to be inordinately fond of pearls and collected them and watched over them, as did the Naga-kings in their great submarine palaces. It was even said that dragons stole the pearly eyes of fishes, which is why dead fish washed ashore are usually eyeless. Given the dragons' greed for pearls, what could be more likely than that they would attempt to acquire the greatest pearl of them all, and, sure enough, an eclipse of the moon was said to be caused by a dragon who had at last succeeded in swallowing it. So on a stormy night dragon-shaped clouds can be seen continually to chase, snatch at, swallow and disgorge the moon.

This explanation seems totally satisfactory until you consider the possibility that the pearl actually symbolizes the sun, as some authorities categorically state. This would explain why it is sometimes represented as a fiery ball, the 'lightning flashes' being, in fact, flames. The idea that some monstrous creature swallows the sun each evening and belches it forth at dawn is an ancient one, and also storm and rain clouds can be seen to obliterate the sun by day as surely as they obliterate the moon by night (although some of the authorities who call the pearl the sun say that the dragon is not actually attempting to capture it, but is gazing at it in the hope of learning the secret of its brilliance so that he may arrange to glow with similar fire himself). One of the strongest arguments of all is based on the appearance of the huge Chinese New Year Dragon, traditionally made of linen, bamboo and paper, which is borne in procession through the streets in pursuit of a red ball which is carried on a stick just ahead of him. It is suggested that this dragon represents the constellation of Draco, and that the head of this constellation used, at one time, to draw nightly nearer to the setting point of the sun until, at New Year, it rose at the actual point of the sunset, as if it had long pursued and finally captured the red ball at

Right *Mother-of-pearl inlay on a late eighteenth-century piece of furniture from Vietnam shows two dragons pursuing the pearl, portrayed here as the interlocking symbol of yin and yang, the negative-feminine and the positive-masculine life forces. This emblem of the dual influence of nature is present in the dragon image itself.*

the horizon. But no sooner is this explanation grasped than another authority points out that it is the appearance of the moon just before the rising of the dragon stars that announces the coming of the Chinese New Year, and the likelihood of the pearl being the sun diminishes once more.

To see the pearl as rolling thunder, the moon or the sun is to see it as a symbol of physical reality, but the dragon itself had spiritual as well as physical significance, and a strong case can be made for the pearl symbolizing the egg emblem of the dual influences of nature. Possibly the best known of all Chinese art motifs is the interlocking black and white symbol of yin and yang, the negative-feminine and the positive-masculine life forces. Another way of representing these two complementary energies is to show the egg being entered by the spermatozoa, and a biological diagram of this event looks remarkably like the round pearl with its bean-shoot-like appendage. The dragon, the spirit of change and of life itself, pursues and plays with the symbol of the two forces whose fluctuating energies are at the root of all change, all life.

The second of the more mystical interpretations of the symbol says that it is the 'pearl of potentiality', the loss of which foredooms deficient power – it is a symbol of wisdom, of enlightenment, of self-realization, of spiritual richness, which is always within sight of the life force but which often eludes it. This view of the pearl as truth or spiritual life is generally taken to be the most satisfactory explanation of its meaning, and it does not exclude the possibility that the pearl is also the moon, which shares the same symbolic attributes. If the pearl and the moon are both the external form of an internal truth, it is understandable that the dragon in his search for wisdom and immortality would reach out to grasp them.

The dragon's objective is hard to define in words because it is a symbol, and symbols are used precisely because words are inadequate or clumsy. In the same way the symbol of the dragon himself is hard to define, but here some of the confusion may arise because there are in China various different types of dragon, each with slightly different aims and appearances.

In *Outlines of Chinese Symbolism and Art Motives*, C.A.S. Williams says:

> A primitive form of dragon is known as *k'vei*. It is a beneficent creature, said to exert a restraining influence against the sin of greed and it generally occurs in conventional form on ancient Chinese bronzes. Other varieties are the Celestial Dragon, which protects and supports the mansions of the gods; the Spiritual Dragon which produces wind and rain to benefit mankind; the Dragon of Hidden Treasures which mounts guard over the wealth concealed from mortal eyes; the Winged Dragon; the Horned Dragon; the Coiling Dragon, which inhabits the waters; and the Yellow Dragon, which emerged from the River Lo to present the elements of writing to the legendary emperor Fu Hsi.

Williams also says that there are nine offshoots of the dragon which are described in the *Ch'ien Chu'eh Lei Shu* of Ch'en Jen Hsi as follows:

> The *P'u-lao*, carved at the tops of bells and gongs, in token of its habit of crying out loudly when attacked by its arch-enemy the whale; the *Ch'iu-niu*, carved on the screws of fiddles, owing to its taste for music; the *Pi-hsi*, carved on the top of stone tablets, since

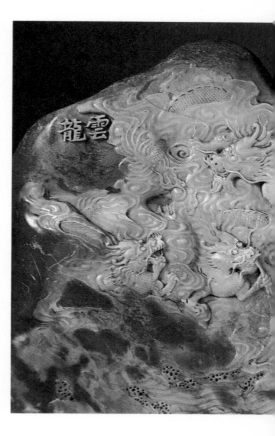

Above *Dragons (yang) in clouds (yin) pursuing the pearl on a Ch'ing dynasty soapstone (eighteenth century). Both Taoism and Buddhism speak of a 'divine pearl' or a 'moon pearl', and the Nagas certainly possessed the 'precious pearl which grants all desires'.*

it was fond of literature; the *Pa-hsia*, carved at the bottom of stone monuments, as it was able to support heavy weights; the *Chao-feng*, carved on the eaves of temples, owing to its liking for danger; the *Chih-wen*, carved on the beams of bridges, because of its fondness for water. It is also placed on the roofs of buildings to keep off fire. It likes to gaze and look out, and is sometimes symbolised by the figure of a fish with uplifted tail; the *Suan-ni*, carved on Buddha's throne, on account of its propensity for resting. It has also been identified with the *Shih-tzu* or symbolic lion; the *Yai-tzu*, carved on sword hilts, and where the blade joins the handle, in memory of its lust for slaughter; the *Pi-kan*, carved on prison gates, as it was addicted to litigation and quarrelling, and loved to use its energy and strength, being very fierce. It is a scaly beast with one horn.

These nine are sometimes called the nine sons of the true dragon. But there are more dragons even than this. There is the *Yu lung*, or fish dragon, which illustrates the metamorphosis of carp into dragon. Legend says that when a carp has succeeded in leaping the cataracts called the Dragon Gate in the Yang-tze river, its reward is to be transformed into a dragon and made immortal. In China the carp is the symbol of aspiration, and colleges sometimes took the fish dragon as an emblem because the passing of exams was seen as the human equivalent of the leaping of the cataracts.

And there is the Dragon-horse, which is the same as the Yellow Dragon. It is seen as a benevolent horse, with scales and wings, which lives in all rivers but especially the Lo, and which emerges from the water with a map on its back whenever a holy man is on the throne. Its most celebrated emergence was to offer the secret of writing to Fu Hsi, the first of the Ten Emperors, although some say that what it actually offered were the 'diagrams used in divination' or, in other words, the eight trigrams of the *I Ching*. It is the relationship of the trigrams to each other that is

Below *Dragons, known as Chih-wen, were placed on the roofs of buildings in Vietnam as guardians, to ward off fire. This may be connected with the idea that dragons were rain-makers.*

important in divination – but their eight basic meanings are as follows: heaven; earth; thunder; water, clouds; mountain; wind; sun, lightning fire; and lake. An ancient Chinese saying goes: 'In heaven a horse is made into a dragon, and among men a dragon is made into a horse.'

Other authorities say that there are only four kinds of dragon – the *T'ien lung* or Celestial Dragon; the *Shen-lung* or spiritual dragon who holds sway over the winds and rain; the *Ti-lung* or dragon of the earth, with powers over rivers and streams; and the *Fu-ts'ang lung*, or dragon of hidden treasure. Of all these dragons, the Spirit Dragon, the *Shen-lung*, was the most important and is the dragon most frequently depicted in art. The variation in the number of claws visible on the feet of the Spirit Dragon denotes the different ranks held by one creature, rather than denoting different creatures. The Chinese Imperial Dragon always has five claws and is found only on imperial insignia and accoutrements. The ordinary plebian dragon has four claws, and if an ordinary man designed himself a five-clawed dragon he was inviting the death penalty. Early Chinese dragons and most Japanese dragons have three claws.

In Japan the dragon is called *Tatsu*, and is generally more serpentine than the Chinese dragon. Rain was not such a problem in Japan and so prayers for it were rare. The dragon was seen more as a sea-god, though he was also a river god and there is some evidence that human sacrifices were made to river dragons. There are many stories of mysterious lights in Japan, most of which move through the woods or from the woods to the sea, and which are variously explained as natural gases or clouds of fireflies. But there is one inexplicable mysterious light which is said to arise in the sea and to fly from there to the mountains, where it hangs in an old pine tree outside one of the Buddhist temples. It is called the Dragon Lantern and is supposedly an offering sent by the dragons of the sea to the deities of the shrines.

The dragon in Japan is quite a complex creature because, as Buddhism grew stronger there, so the original Japanese dragons began to resemble the Indian Nagas. What is more, the tales of the Indian Nagas came to Japan by way of China so that the Japanese dragon became something of a mongrel. The Indian Nagas, although serpentine, were sufficiently dragon-like to interbreed, at least mythologically, with the Chinese, and later the Japanese, dragons. Serpent worship in its various forms existed in India long before Buddhism and, to some extent, still exists today, and the Naga cult was one of its manifestations. In his *Dragons and Dragon-lore*, Ernest Ingersoll describes them as 'demi-gods in various serpentine forms, uncertain of temper and fearful in possibilities of harm, whose "kings" lived in luxury in magnificent palaces in the depths of the sea or at the bottom of inland lakes'.

The Nagas were water-deities. They were sometimes associated with sacred pools or wells, in which case they were presumed to live underwater at the base of an adjacent tree; and were sometimes sea-gods. Their palaces were opulent and beautiful and often took the form of whole cities, encrusted with jewels, where they occasionally entertained men who managed to find their way there. In art and iconography, Nagas are represented sometimes as gigantic snakes, often multi-headed, and sometimes in human form with either a crown of snakes, snakes growing from their necks, or else as snakes from the waist down. There are supposedly four types of Naga. There are the Heavenly Nagas, who uphold and guard the heavenly palaces; Divine Nagas who cause clouds to rise and rain to fall; Earthly Nagas who clear out and drain off rivers; and Hidden Nagas who are the guardians of treasure.

When the evangelical cult of Buddhism was spreading in India, serpent-worship was one of its chief problems. But the Mahayana school or Greater Vehicle which dominated Buddhism for eight centuries from about the birth of Christ, was tolerant of the serpent-worship and, unlike Christianity, did not try to quash the older cults but absorbed them, eventually persuading the Nagas into the service of the Buddha. The Nagas had always been regarded as capable of raising clouds and thunder whenever they were angry with humanity and the Mahayana school reinterpreted this as the power of bestowing life-giving rain. So the Nagas became as benevolent as Chinese dragons.

There is a story that, immediately after his enlightenment, the Buddha went to Lake Mucilinda and meditated there for seven days. The Naga of

Below An Imperial dragon, characterized by five claws, embroidered on a mandarin robe of the Ch'ing dynasty. Any commoner who dared to design a dragon with five, rather than four claws, was sentenced to death.

Left *A* famille verte *dish, depicting the spring fishing festival with the dragon representing the ruler of the watery deep.*

the lake saw the Buddha's light and rose to the surface, where he was so delighted that he caused it to rain for the whole seven days and protected the sage by curling his seven hoods, or heads, over him.

Nevertheless, there were still ferocious Nagas as well as devout ones, just as there always had been. Long before Buddhism, Vishnu, the supreme being, had had an ambiguous relationship with serpents, killing the serpent-demons and riding the serpent-eating Garuda, but also sleeping on a serpent-bed beneath the ocean. And an element of this ambiguity remained. When Buddhism reached China, where there are no cobras, and when the pictures which included Nagas therefore lost their impact and began to be repainted to include the familiar dragons, these dragons were often given Naga-like attributes, which sometimes included an almost demonic expression.

The Garuda was a gigantic divine bird who became the steed of Vishnu. In Vedic times the Garuda was entirely eagle, although he was represented in partly human form later. Garudas lived on snakes and were therefore the deadly enemies of the Nagas. Later, even a Chinese dragon could be frightened into making rain if it was threatened with a Garuda. Gradually Vishnu, who was an early sky-god, lost his place as head of the Indian pantheon and became one of the ten *dikpalas* who reigned in and over water. As lord of the waters he was also lord of the Nagas, and yet his mount, the Garuda, was their enemy. In *The Indian Theogony*, Sukamari Bhattacharji says: 'These two aspects of Vishnu, his Garuda manifestation and his relationship with the serpent are found together in the Mexican god Quetzalcoatl . . . .'

The dragons, like the Nagas, are often spoken of expressly as mythical beings, as symbols of spiritual or meteorological import, but they are also spoken of, frequently in works which quote far older works, as if they were creatures which actually existed. For instance, de Visser quotes from an unnamed Chinese work, '... there was Shuh Ngan of Liu who had a distant descendant called Tung Fu, very fond of dragons, and able to find out their tastes and likings, so as to supply them with drink and meat. Many dragons sought refuge with him and he reared the dragons according to their nature in order to serve the Emperor Shun, who gave him the name of Tung and the family name of Hwan-lung (dragon rearer).'

The existence of truly ancient books in Chinese has always been in some doubt. But in *Mythical Monsters* (1886), Charles Gould says:

> As it is well known that all the ancient books, with the exception of those on medicine, divination and husbandry, were ordered to be destroyed in the year 212 BC by the Emperor Tsin Shi Hwang Ti, under the threatened penalty for non-compliance of branding and labour on the walls for four years, and that a persecution of the *literati* was commenced by him in the succeeding year, which resulted in the burying alive in pits of four hundred and sixty of their number, it may be reasonably objected that the claims to high antiquity which some of the Chinese classics put forth are, to say the least, doubtful, and in some instances, highly improbable.

This question has been well considered by Mr Legge in his valuable translation of the Chinese Classics. He points out that the

Below In Hindu mythology Vishnu is described lying motionless on a thousand-headed cobra, which floats on an ocean of milk. The ocean represents totality, uniformity and stillness. The serpent, called Ananta, is eternity. Lakshmi, Vishnu's wife, goddess of abundance and harmony, is in attendance. The lotus-flower from Vishnu's navel holds Brahma, the first divine shape with an active role to play in the creation. Each of his four arms holds a book, and from his four mouths he reads the eternal laws, the Vedas. This painting is from the Kangra district, the centre of Rajput miniature painting in the nineteenth century.

tyrant died within three years of the burning of the books, and that the Han dynasty was founded only eleven years after that date, in 201 BC, shortly after which attempts were commenced to recover the ancient literature. He concludes that vigorous efforts to carry out the edict would not be continued longer than the life of its author – that is, not for more than three years – and that the materials from which the classics, as they come down to us, were compiled and edited in the two centuries preceding the Christian era, were genuine remains, going back to a still more remote period.

These ancient books, then, do talk of the taming and breeding of dragons and of their use in drawing the chariots of emperors, and it is extremely hard to see what kind of animal could have been meant, certainly not the snake. Probably the stories were simply intended to show that the emperor, in his glory, could even command the weather itself, in the form of the weather deities.

It is not only ancient books, though, which talk of dragons as real, living animals. In *A Dictionary of Chinese Mythology* by E.T.C. Werner, which was originally published in Shanghai in 1932, a dragon appearance was recorded for 1931, which, in terms of the age of the majority of dragon stories, is relatively recent. Werner says:

> The following incident, which occurred in May 1931, indicates the persistence of the beliefs above noted [beliefs in dragons]. A scaled and horned dragon, believed by many to be a supernatural creature, has made its appearance in Kiangsi, the communist-ridden province, according to a letter from Mr Huang Wen-Chih, formerly President of the Hankow General Chamber of Commerce.
>
> Mr Huang writes from Nangchang saying that the dragon was seen on the Kan River, the principal river in Kiangsi, about half a month ago. He adds that the presence of the dragon is the cause of the flood between Nangchang and Feng-chang, which are some 200 *li* apart. Most of the houses in that region have been inundated during the past two weeks.
>
> As the Book of History recorded that some 2,000 years ago the people used to offer the fairest maiden every year to the Ho Po, or God of the River, to be his concubine, it is now suggested that some suitable sacrifice should be presented to the dragon. It is said that if his wrath is appeased, the flood will subside. On the other hand, if nothing is done to please the creature, it would make the Kiangsi people suffer more besides the flood and the communist uprisings.

There is no record as to whether or not the dragon eventually received a sacrifice.

It is also interesting to think of the 12 animals of the Chinese zodiac which dates from 2637 BC. They are the rat, the ox, the tiger, the hare, the dragon, the serpent, the horse, the sheep, the monkey, the cock, the dog and the boar. Not only is it clear that there was then no confusion between serpents and dragons, but also the dragon is the only one of the 12 which, apparently, cannot be readily encountered in the flesh today.

To encounter almost any Chinese dragon would be a rare privilege, an excellent omen for one's future, and an aesthetic pleasure. To encounter a Western dragon would be an entirely different experience.

Below *Buddha, after his Enlightenment, went to Lake Mucilinda and meditated for seven days. The Naga of the lake saw Buddha's light and rose to the surface and caused it to rain for 7 days, protecting the sage with his 7 hoods. This statue of the Buddha is in Angkor Wat style, twelfth-century.*

Western Dragons

With few exceptions, the dragons of the West are heavy, evil, earthbound and hideous, the complete antithesis of the airy, benevolent, elegant dragons of the East. Because almost all the Western dragon stories are Christian in origin, the biblical view predominates, and although dragons vary slightly from place to place, the cave-dwelling, fire-breathing, pestilential and destructive creature of the North and West had his character formed in the Old Testament and in the Revelations of St John the Divine, where he appears either as a form of the devil himself or as a symbol of desolation, both spiritual and physical.

Prophesies of the destruction of Babylon promise that the awful Babylonian dragon will inherit the city: 'And thorns shall come up in her palaces, nettles and brambles in the fortresses thereof: And it shall be an habitation of dragons, and a court for owls.' (Isaiah XXXIV, 13). The dragon's first appearance as a symbol of the tempting devil is in the Garden of Eden in one of the best-known, earliest and most emotive of biblical stories. Of this appearance P.B. Lum, in *Fabulous Beasts*, says: '. . . it is thought possible that the curse laid on the serpent in the Old Testament was an attempt to discredit a powerful dragon-serpent cult that was flourishing when the Jewish religion was first formulated.' And in the Revelation of St John XII, 1–9, the terrible appearance and significance of the dragon reach their peak.

Right *This thirteenth-century English manuscript shows the Child being drawn up safely to heaven while the dragon, who had hoped to devour it, watches impotently. (Bodleian Library Ms. Tanner 184 P. 164K/10)*

1. And there appeared a great wonder in heaven; a woman clothed with the sun, and the moon under her feet, and upon her head a crown of twelve stars:

2. And she being with child cried, travailing in birth, and pained to be delivered.

3. And there appeared another wonder in heaven; and behold a great red dragon, having seven heads and ten horns, and seven crowns upon his heads.

4. And his tail drew the third part of the stars of heaven, and did cast them to the earth: and the dragon stood before the woman which was ready to be delivered, for to devour her child as soon as it was born.

5. And she brought forth a man child, who was to rule all nations with a rod of iron: and her child was caught up unto God, and to his throne.

6. And the woman fled into the wilderness, where she hath a place prepared of God, that they should feed her there a thousand two hundred and threescore days.

7. And there was war in heaven: Michael and his angels fought against the dragon; and the dragon fought and his angels,

8. And prevailed not; neither was their place found any more in heaven.

9. And the great dragon was cast out, that old serpent, called the Devil, and Satan, which deceiveth the whole world: he was cast out into the earth, and his angels were cast out with him.

Above A fourteenth-century tapestry from Angers in France showing the seven-headed dragon, beast of the Apocalypse, the devil and the sixth angel. The image of the frog coming out of the mouth of the dragon occurs in many alchemical treatises as a symbol of preliminary forms.

And later in the same chapter comes the warning: 'And the dragon was wroth with the woman, and went to make war with the remnant of her seed, which keep the commandments of God, and have the testimony of Jesus Christ.'

In the early days of literacy, the Bible was the most widely-read work, closely followed in popularity by the Bestiaries, which were in common circulation in the Middle Ages. The first Bestiary, known as the *Physiologus*, is of unknown authorship, but it is generally accepted that it originated in Alexandria. The title means The Naturalist, which is misleading to our eyes today because both it and the later Bestiaries were written in a less scientific age than ours, when large areas of the world were unexplored and when the appearance and habits of even the commonest creatures were not catalogued with much precision. A Bestiary usually described the habits and appearance of about 40 creatures, some real and some mythical, and was likely to be illustrated with illuminated miniatures. The supposedly scientific descriptions were not only usually incorrect, but were also considered far less important than the moral lesson which was attached to each creature. The Bestiary was valued as an improving, religious and moralistic work, and had in many ways the same flavour as the much later fables of Aesop and La Fontaine. Although the Bestiaries did differ, one from another, the symbolism of the creatures described rarely changed; the pelican was always the symbol of purity and mother-love, feeding her young with drops of blood plucked from her own breast, the phoenix was always the symbol of resurrection, the panther always signified Jesus Christ, to whom all other animals were drawn by the sweetness of its breath and nature, and the dragon was always the anti-Christ, the one beast who eschewed the panther.

However, even though the Bestiary was understood to be above all things an 'improving work', the scientific descriptions of the creatures were taken seriously because it was from the supposed real-life behaviour of the creatures that their specific moral roles grew. The Bestiary purported to be allegory based on fact and therefore the descriptions of the dragons' behaviour, habitat and very existence would be believed and medieval cartographers, for instance, would place dragons on maps in the areas indicated by the Bestiaries.

One of the best known of these books was the *Bestaire de Guillaume le Clerc de Normandie*, which was compiled in 1210–11. The following quotations come from a translation by George Claridge Druce, published in Kent in 1936. First comes the symbolic meaning of the dragon, which is shown as the devil, and then the scientific description of the dragon:

Below *Two sections from a fourteenth-century altar-piece, attributed to Master Bertram of Hamburg. The first shows the dragon's mouth as the entrance to hell: 'And I looked, and behold a pale horse: and his name that sat on him was Death, and Hell followed with him', Rev. 6:8. The second shows the seven-headed beast of Revelations.*

> Now it is right that we tell you
> Of the form of the dragon.
> Of all the beasts which creep
> Is the dragon far the biggest.
> The real dragon – it is found
> In the kingdom of Ethiopia.
> It has a little mouth and a big body;
> In the air it glows like fine gold.
> It has a long tail and great crest.
> Great trouble it makes for the elephant,
> For with its tail it strikes it

In the legs so that it throws it down;
It bears no deadly poison,
But is vastly big and strong,
And with its tail it scourges
Everything within its reach;
Nor does it do great hurt
Save with its tail only.

The impact made on medieval minds by the stories in the Bible and the Bestiaries was reinforced by early European, and especially English and Norwegian, church architecture, where the use of emblems and symbolic carvings and paintings was regarded as an essential part of the education of a largely illiterate population. The Temptation of Eve was a favourite subject, since it was the Fall that made the redemption necessary, and the serpent is sometimes expressly depicted as a dragon on fonts and misericords. The Triumph of St Michael, in which the dragon is sometimes a reptile and sometimes a demonic human figure, also appears often, and so does the ancient story of the dragon attacking the doves which feed on the Tree of Life. In *Symbolism of Animals and Birds represented in English Church Architecture*, Arthur Collins says:

> This tree is supposed to grow in India: doves lodge in its branches and eat its sweet fruit. The dragon is afraid of the tree, and flees to whichever side is not in its shadow. If a dove ventures beyond the tree the dragon devours it. The symbolism of the story is as follows: the tree is God; the shadow is the Son; the Dove is the Holy Spirit, and also it seems the Christian; and the fruit of the tree represents wisdom.

There is no need to spell out the symbolic meaning of the dragon!
The Norwegian wooden stave churches also kept the image of the

49

Right *A Norwegian stave church with dragons and crosses on the ridge beams of the roof. The dragon image was kept alive in the Middle Ages to remind the people that base emotions (the dragon) had to be overcome to achieve high Christian ideals.*

Left *Medieval bestiaries tell us that doves live in the Perindeus tree because they love its fruit. The dragon is an enemy of the dove, but fears the tree it lives in and the shadow it casts. However, if a dove leaves the tree, the dragon will eat it. This can be interpreted as the tree being God the Father, the shade, God the Son, and the dove, the Christian who has received the Holy Ghost. If the Christian leaves the refuge of God, the dragon (the devil) will devour him.*

Below *An elaborately carved wooden post in the form of a dragon's head from a Viking ship burial site at Oseberg. Fearsome images at burial sites were believed to have been placed there for the protection of the dead (c.850 AD).*

dragon firmly before people's eyes. Apart from the dragon heads on the outside corner beams, most of the dragons and snakes which appear are specifically those of the Nibelung Saga. In *Stave Churches in Norway* Dan Lindholm says: 'The pagan world of heroes, gradually sinking into the twilight of the gods, went hand in hand for several centuries with a form of Christianity not yet grasped intellectually. Sigurd, the conqueror of the dragon, and the Risen Christ – both had their appropriate place in the stave churches.' The place of the dragon was the inferior one; he was clearly the degenerative and negative force, dragging man down, which must be overcome if the message of the risen Christ was to be understood in any way, intellectually or emotionally. The doors of stave churches are so narrow that only one person can pass through at a time, so that entry into the body of the church has to be a thoughtful and personal experience. And the door frames tend to be carved with a multiplicity of dragons and snakes, perhaps, Lindholm suggests, as a reminder of the tangled thoughts and lower, dragon-nature that should be overcome on entering the church.

Hardly surprising, then, that the dragon was seen as eminently slayable, and that several saints, as well as Michael himself, were reputed to have slain, tamed, or otherwise overcome this dragon or its progeny, in many of its manifestations, including flood, because the old association with water, and especially with inundation, remained unbroken.

The Western attitude to the dragon is perhaps best illustrated by the legend of St George who is such a famous dragon-slayer that he almost eclipses St Michael. St Michael threw the dragon out of heaven and left St George to deal with him once he landed on earth; and so it is not so much that Michael is less important as that he is too important. Impossible to identify with such a High Saint but quite possible to identify with a human man, canonized as a martyr.

The standard *Dictionary of Saints*, compiled by Donald Attwater, has the following entry:

George, St, Martyr: There is reason to believe that St George was a martyr who suffered at Diospolis (Lydda, Ludd) in Palestine, probably before the time of Constantine; beyond this there seems nothing that can be affirmed with confidence. He is the subject of numerous legends, of which the dragon story is a comparatively late one. The East revered him in early times as a patron of soldiers and he was known in England long before he was adopted as her patron in the late Middle Ages; he was declared to be Protector of the Kingdom of England by Pope Benedict XIV.

Because historical details have proved elusive, the actual existence of St George as an historical figure has frequently been cast into doubt, and his identity confused with that of another man from the same area, George of Cappadocia (d. 361) (a title which, because of the general confusion, is often bestowed on St George himself). This confusion was initiated by Edward Gibbon in his *The Decline and Fall of the Roman Empire*. Having described the life and acts of George of Cappadocia, a heretic Bishop who was so corrupt, barbaric and tyrannical that he was expelled from the bishopric and eventually torn to pieces by an enraged mob, he says: 'The meritorious death of the archbishop obliterated the memory of his life', and points out that the Arian heretics hailed this George as the saint. 'The odious stranger, disguising every circumstance of time and place, assumed the mask of a martyr, a saint and a Christian hero; and the infamous George of Cappadocia has been transformed into the renowned St George of England, the patron of arms, of chivalry, and of the garter.' The Arians hailed as a saint a man who had persecuted the Catholics, but it is unlikely that the Holy Roman Church would feel the same way about him. In any case, dedications to St George the Martyr, found in Syria, have proved to date from a time when Bishop George was still alive.

Whether or not George ever existed, and the true George still has his place in the Roman Catholic and Anglican Church Calendars, he quickly became a folk hero of immense power and gathered to himself all kinds of stories, including one which gave him English parentage, a belief to which even Spenser seems to subscribe in *The Faërie Queene*. He seems to have had a strong grasp on the imagination of the English even before he superseded Edward the Confessor as patron saint, and certainly before Richard I claimed him as protector of himself and his army just before the Third Crusade.

In 1631, Peter Heylin published his meticulously researched *The History of St George of Cappadocia*, in which he sought 'to cleere the history of St George from all further questions'. In this book he discusses Peter Comester, the so-called 'Father of the Fabulous Tales and Legends current in the Roman Church', who was writing about 1150 and whose work may have been the source of some of the legends. However the most famous legend of all, that of the fight with the dragon, is a relatively late one and as principal source of this legend Heylin cites James, Archbishop of Genoa, who was writing in 1280.

Right This woodcut by Albrecht Dürer shows St Michael and his angels casting 'that old serpent', the dragon or devil, out of heaven.

St George of Cappadocia, a Colonell or a Tribune of the Soldiers at that time, came to the country of Libya, and to the Citie of Sisena (A city, as Don Quixote said of his kingdome errant, that is not to bee found in all the Map). Neere to this Towne, there was a

Lake as big as any Sea, God blesse us, and in that Lake a deadly Dragon, which with his breath did poyson all the Country round about him; and therefore the poore people were compel'd, God helpe em, to give him every day two sheepe, to keepe him quiet. At last, when all their sheepe were spent, alas poore people, they were compell'd to give him every day one sheepe, and one man or one woman with it, to make up the number. And then when almost all their Sonnes and Daughters had been eaten, at length the cruell and unlucky lot fell upon the Kings Daughter, her Fathers onely Child, and her mothers blessing. It was a sorry house, I warrant you, but who could helpe it, the poore Lady was drawne forth into the Fields, and stript of all her gay attire, and bound unto a stake, and ready for the foule Feind that was to eate her . . . .

At this stage, despite the fact that he does not doubt for one moment the existence of the true George, Heylin makes the point that the rest of the tale is exactly that of Perseus and Andromeda as told by Ovid in his *Metamorphoses*, and indeed many people insist that the entire story may have come from that source.

Whatever its source, the story continues, saying that George, passing by, saw the king's daughter, weeping and bound, and enquired what was the trouble. She told him, and warned him to run for his life, since there was no point in both of them being eaten. In these early tellings of the

Above *The story of the Red Cross Knight in Spenser's* Faerie Queene *tells how*
'The Knight with that old Dragon fights
two days incessantly:
The third him overthrowes, and gayns
most glorious victory.'
The Red Cross Knight is St George, but, in a reverse of the usual story, here he is fighting to rescue the aged parents of his beloved from the tower wherein the dragon has imprisoned them.

Right *Many dragons were reputed to come from Ethiopia, and here St George is killing the dragon in a seventeenth-century Ethiopian manuscript of the Four Gospels.*

story she was always brave and determined, only much later, as the Age of Chivalry advanced, did she become fearful and clinging. However, George stood his ground and pinned the advancing dragon to the earth with his lance. In most versions, the dragon was then bound with the princess's girdle and led back to the city where it was killed in view of the people. Because George insisted that his strength came from Christ, first the princess and then the entire population were baptized as Christians. In this case, the dragon may well have symbolized pagan belief, from which the mortal soul of the princess and all her people were at last delivered by the man of God.

George is said to have been martyred for trampling on an anti-Christian edict issued by the Emperor Diocletian (245–313), which had been pinned to a wall, and which George tore down and trod underfoot. The catalogue of his torments, which has been elaborated down the years, makes sickening reading, and the very fact that he supposedly survived a series of tortures any one of which would have killed a mortal man, puts his story in doubt in the minds of many people.

Despite the doubts, though, the general consensus of opinion seems to be that, although his story has been lavishly embellished, George did exist and was martyred. It is even possible that he encountered a dragon. According to popular legend, the famous conflict took place in Beirut and, according to the accounts of crusaders, the swamps and estuaries of the surrounding areas teemed with crocodiles. But in many ways the historical reality of George is irrelevant. It is the eagerness of people to believe in, and to embellish, the dragon legend that is interesting. By then the dragon as the embodiment of danger and evil existed as an idea, and the idea of a saviour to slay it was already hovering in people's minds, ready to fall upon the shoulders of any likely hero, or, indeed, heroine.

Michael and George were dragon-slayers in the grand style, whose activities were the inspiration for a great number of works of art, but dragon legends became attached to the lives of other saints as well.

St Martha's dragon, the Tarasque, was almost certainly a flood, although he may have been a heresy because the heretical sect of Cathars came from the same area. He lived in the Rhone, in the region of Aix, and ravaged the countryside until Martha quelled him by sprinkling him with holy water, binding him with her girdle and leading him to the people, who themselves killed him.

Not every dragon was totally evil, and St Simeon's dragon is more likely to have stood for redeemable sin than for the spirit of all evil. St Simeon Stylites, the son of a Sicilian shepherd, is the best known of the so-called pillar saints. He became a monk when he was hardly more than a child, lived as a hermit for some years, and acquired such a reputation for purity, austerity and wisdom that people flocked to him. To avoid them, he elected to live on a platform on top of a pillar at Telanessa near Antioch. The first pillar was about three metres (ten feet) high but, as his unusual way of life aroused ever more admiration and brought ever more pilgrims to his feet, he gradually increased the height until it was about 18 metres (60 feet). When he died in 495 he had lived on his pillar for 37 years.

In his attempts to rise above humanity, St Simeon drew not only crowds of people but also, according to legend, a dragon. One of the earliest tellings of his story was in *Vita* by Antonius, *c*.330, and it has been translated by Helen Waddell in her collection *Beasts and Saints*:

Above *St Margaret, patron saint of childbirth, was said to have been the daughter of a heathen priest of Antioch, but was converted to Christianity by her nurse. The Governor of Antioch asked her to be his wife, but she refused. He was so angry that he imprisoned her in a dungeon. A devil appeared to her in the form of a dragon and swallowed her whole. The dragon burst and St Margaret emerged alive, only to be beheaded by the Governor.*

Above *The first part of the story of St George from a fifteenth-century altar-piece attributed to Marzas de Sas (c.1410), showing the child being fed to the dragon with distraught onlookers, including the king and queen. St George arrives when the only person left to offer the dragon is the princess. He rescues her, kills the dragon, and in some versions of the story, marries her.*

Now at that time there was an exceedingly large dragon that lived close by, in the country to the north: and because of him no grass ever grew there: and a branch of a tree fell into his right eye. And lo, one day the blind dragon came, dragging himself along, and he applied himself to the pillar which was the habitation of the man of God, and winding himself into a wheel as if to ask pardon, lay with his head bowed low. And the blessed Simeon gazed down upon him, and straightway, the branch fell out of his eye: and it was a cubit in length. And indeed all that saw it glorified God, notwithstanding that they fled from him in terror. But the creature coiled itself up and stayed quiet in one place, whilst all the people went by. Then rising up, it worshipped at the gate of the monastery for well nigh two hours, and so returned to its den, and did no hurt to any.

Other saints have shown their compassion for all life by helping sick animals, but in this case the specific problem may have been symbolic – blind sin was able to see God by the intercession of a holy man. On the other hand it is just possible that the story evolved to help to explain an ouroboros; the coiled figure of a dragon carved around a pillar.

The Western dragon was evil, but could always be overcome by the power of the cross; dangerous though it was, it was no match for faith, piety and courage. Because of this, despite its ability to persecute the gullible with fear and dread, a meeting with a dragon was almost something to be wished for as an opportunity to prove oneself. In 1916, many long years after belief in dragons had faded, H.D.C. Pepler summed up the attitude of the West in a poem for children, privately printed at Ditchling in Sussex:

CHILD
Are *all* the dragons fled?
Are all the goblins dead?
Am I *quite* safe in bed?

NURSE
Thou art quite safe in bed
Dragons and goblings all are dead.

CHILD
When Michael's angels fought
The dragon, was it caught?
Did it jump and *roar*?
(Oh, nurse don't shut the door).
And did it try to bite?
(Nurse don't blow out the light).

NURSE
Hush, thou knowest what I said,
Saints and dragons all are dead.

FATHER
(To himself)
O child, nurse lies to thee,
For dragons thou shalt see.
Please God that on that day
Thou may'st a dragon slay.
And if thou do'st not faint
God shall not want a Saint.

Plumed Serpents
and Lake Monsters

The theme of the conflict between hero and dragon does not seem to predominate in New World mythology, but it is there. North American Indian creation myths often mention a serpentine spirit of the waters who opposed the creator in his work, and South American stories tell of the gigantic serpent who swallows the sun each night and disgorges it at dawn. Certainly, there are dragons. In the North they principally take the form of the *genus locii* of lakes, but in Mexico and South America they are rather different. There the dragon is the plumed serpent in which the feathered bird of the sky and the scaled snake of the earth unite.

The serpent, which does of course exist as a physical reality in these countries, had at least four symbolic meanings, none of them really contradictory. It was a symbol of strength, of wisdom, of the earth as opposed to the sky, and of time. The Maya symbol of a pair of serpents with their tails intertwined and their heads directed outwards represents time and eternity, the space-time continuum. The number 4, associated with the Maya plumed serpent, was sacred throughout the Americas because it represented the four quarters of the earth and, later, the four elements. Further, the snake has long been believed to hold the secret of immortality because of its ability to cast its skin and so renew itself. Life was understood to be cyclic, the sun set and rose again, plants died back and then burgeoned forth, but the snake was the only living creature seen to contain a series of cycles within its own lifetime.

In *Mexican and Central American Mythology*, Irene Nicholson describes the feathered serpent as 'the soul taking wings to heaven, and ... matter descending to earth as the crawling snake,' and adds a tantalizing comment: 'One South American statesman – now many years dead – told a journalist who was searching for a solution to his country's problems that Latin America would discover and fulfil her true destiny only when the plumed serpent learned to fly.'

Various suggestions have been put forward to explain the origins of this particular composite dragon, who is perhaps best-known as Quetzal-coatl of Mexico. Irene Nicholson gives a detailed breakdown of the name, explaining that it is

> ... made up of *quetzal*, a rare bird with green feathers inhabiting the highlands of Chiapas and Guatemala, living in the tops of trees, rarely visible, and distinguished from other birds in having only two front toes and almost no claws; and *coatl*, which is the Nahua word for snake but which is itself a combination of *co*, generic name for serpent or snake in the Maya language, and *atl*, the Nahua word for water.

Below *A detail of a stela from Guatemala showing a priest holding a human head in one hand and the sacrificial knife in the other. The serpents symbolize blood. After some sacrifices, it was believed that the plumed serpent drank the blood of the victim.*

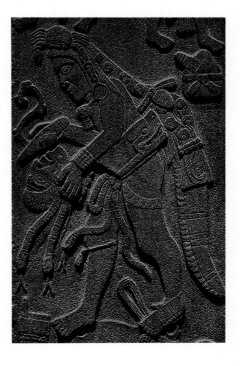

Above *The symmetrical placing of two serpents on this Aztec wood and mosaic mask is somewhat reminiscent of the snakes on the Mercury caduceus. It represents the equilibrium of forces, good balanced by evil, health by sickness.*

Below *A turquoise mosaic pectoral ornament in the form of a double-headed serpent, probably Mixtec workmanship. It is believed to be part of the treasure given by the Aztec ruler Montezuma to Hernando Cortes. The double-headed serpent, the image of duality, occurs throughout dragon/serpent lore.*

Quetzalcoatl is the Mexican equivalent of the Maya Kukulcan, and in *The Fundamental Principles of Old and New World Civilisations*, Zelia Nuttall offers a similar breakdown of this name: '. . . the word *can* means serpent and the numeral four, and is almost homonymous with the word for sky or heaven – *caan*. The image of a serpent, therefore, directly suggested and expressed the idea of something quadruple incorporated in one celestial being and appropriately symbolised the divine ruler of the four quarters.' She adds that both *Ku* and *Kul* are translated as 'divine' or 'holy' so that Kukulcan can be understood to mean 'the divine serpent'. To explain why this divine serpent should be feathered, she says: 'When Mayan sculptors or scribes began to represent this symbol of the divinity they must have searched for some object, easy to depict, the sound of whose name resembled that of Ku or Kul. The Maya adjective "feathered" being *Kukum*, the artists evidently devised the plan of representing, as an effigy of the divinity, a serpent decorated with feathers . . . .' What is more, the feathers depicted are always the precious tail feathers of the quetzal which, apart from being very rare, very beautiful and rather short on toes, had one other unusual attribute – the tail feathers appear, according to the angle of the light, to be blue, red, yellow or green, and these were the colours of the four quarters of the world according to Mexican mythology.

And so all over the Yucatan and Mexico the image of the plumed serpent persists. As one of the aspects of Kukulcan-Quetzalcoatl, he is the subject of monumental stone carvings around the pillars and along the walls of temples and pyramids, which were a source of great puzzlement to early archaeologists.

Quetzalcoatl is a complex figure, and although much has been written about him, it is probable that his essential nature is not really understood today. It is thought that his myth grew around a real man, rather as the Arthurian legend grew in Britain, but no one has yet been able to date this man with any certainty, and estimates vary by thousands of years. The matter is complicated further by the fact that a series of priests and kings adopted the name of this founder of their religion. The historic

Quetzalcoatl is said to have been a great king and religious innovator, wise, good, inventor of a calendar and a law-giver. He is also thought to have originated the blood sacrifice. Initially this was to be blood taken by a supplicant from his own ear or tongue, but eventually the sacrifice idea degenerated until human hearts were offered, cut from a living victim with a knife made of obsidian. He also is credited with pioneering the cultivation of maize as a food crop, and it is this last possibility that sets his date very far back. As such, he is depicted as a human man.

The mythological Quetzalcoatl is also difficult to pin down, partly because stories conflict, and partly because the mythology which contained him was concerned to explain the dualities of existence – life and death, light and dark, spirit and matter. And it is as a mythological being that he is often depicted as the plumed serpent. The serpent is the earth and is physical matter, whereas the feathered bird represents spirit. In this world, each is essential to the other and so Quetzalcoatl, the perfect man, becomes a feathered serpent – duality resolved.

The background to the mythological Quetzalcoatl is similar to the background to other redeeming gods from other times, other places. He had a miraculous birth, of a virgin mother, he was sent to teach mankind and to expiate its sins, he was forced to die and descend to the underworld before he could arise again, triumphant. The complexity of Quetzalcoatl is partly due to his different manifestations. He was seen sometimes as a man and sometimes as a plumed serpent. He was also seen sometimes as the sun and sometimes as the planet Venus. His connection with both planet and sun may partly be explained by the fact that Venus can be seen to disappear into the sun's rays at dawn, suggesting that the planet is eaten by the sun and thereby becomes the sun. When he is depicted pictorially as Venus, Quetzalcoatl is shown being swallowed by a serpent. This serpent represents the earth which, in a sense, can be seen to swallow the planet daily. So the idea of the dark serpent swallowing light appears in South America just as it appears in Egypt and India.

The dragon, or feathered snake, of South America and Mexico is central to the mythology of the region – reptilian, powerful, possibly capable of flight, connected with fertility, with weather phenomena and with the life force, the symbol of resurrection. Although awe-inspiring, it was not an enemy to its own people, no hero was called upon to destroy it, it did not bring pestilence or death, nor did it lay the land to waste. However, symbols are born out of the natures of those who create them, and it would be impossible for the plumed serpent to remain aloof from the gruesome practices that characterized some of the stages of Mexican and Latin American development.

In *The Maya*, Michael Coe talks of the Toltec King, Topiltzin, who ruled in Central Mexico at the time when the Toltecs had just superseded the older civilization there, soon after AD 900. Topiltzin took the title of Quetzalcoatl, or Feathered Serpent. According to some sources, a power-struggle broke out between the peaceful king and his men, and the warrior faction. The king was defeated and sailed away from the Gulf Coast. Michael Coe continues: 'Now it so happens that Maya historical sources speak of the arrival from the West of a man calling himself Kukulcan. (Feathered Serpent) ... who wrested Yucatan from its rightful owners and established his capital at Chichen Itza,' and adds later: 'the archaeological record tells us that the conquest of Yucatan by the

Above *In this green jade Aztec carving the head of Quetzalcoatl, the man, emerges from the jaws of Queltzalcoatl, the plumed serpent.*

Above *In Aztec mythology, Quetzalcoatl is depicted sometimes as a man, and sometimes as a plumed serpent. Here he is again shown in both manifestations, but until Aztec imagery has been fully deciphered, the symbolism remains unclear.*

Below *The double-headed plumed serpent is the dragon of the Maya of Yucatan. The feathered bird of the sky (yang) and the scaled smake of the earth (yin) unite in a representation of eternity.*

supposedly peaceful Topiltzin-Quetzalcoatl and his Toltec armies was violent and brutal in the extreme. The murals found in the Temple of the Warriors at Chichen Itza, and the relief scenes on some golden disks fished up from the Sacred Cenote [natural pool] at the same site, tell the same story. The drama opens with the arrival of the Toltec forces by sea . . . . The final act ends with the heart sacrifice of the Maya leaders, while the Feathered Serpent himself hovers above to receive the bloody offering.' Human sacrifice, and especially the offering of hearts, was a part of serpent worship throughout Central and South America and also in Africa.

Nevertheless, this South American dragon had far more in common with Eastern dragons than with the later Western dragons, and it appears to have had little in common with the North American dragons.

The North American monsters were less powerful, yet they could be destructive. Their habits, their habitats, and the stories which surround them show them to be dragons, but they differ from most other dragons in one important respect. Numerous people, Indians and settlers, have claimed to have seen them, and these claims still arise right up to the present day.

In the North, as in the South, bird and snake were both held to be sacred, and there was a connection between them although they never combined to form one creature. The bird, because of its power of flight, was believed to ascend to heaven, to be the messenger of the gods, to contain the spirits of the dead and to be associated with lightning. (Both lightning and birds of prey can be seen to descend sharply from above and to strike with lethal effectiveness.) Birds, swans in particular, were believed to make the winds, and the sound of thunder was the sound of the cloud bird flapping his wings.

The snake was also associated with lightning, and some mythographers have suggested that that was its paramount meaning. It is certainly true that the movements of both are similar. It has even been suggested that as lightning is golden in colour, gold was believed to be the product of it. If this were ever proved to be universally true it would explain why Nagas, snakes, serpents and dragons are so often associated with a hoard of golden treasure.

Daniel G. Brinton, in his collection *Myths of the New World* (1886), says: 'When Father Buteaux was a missionary among the Algonkins, in 1637, he asked them their opinion of the nature of lightning. "It is an immense serpent", they replied, "which the Manito (creator) is vomiting forth; you can see the twists and folds which he leaves on the trees which he strikes; and underneath such trees we have often found huge snakes".' The snake and the tree have long been associated in both mythology and psychology, so it is not surprising to find the source of the association in reality.

But the lake dragons of the North were more than just snakes. They were, like other dragons, variations on the theme of 'snake'. They were immensely powerful, since they could overturn a boat or drag down a swimmer, and in a more magical way since they could create storms and dangers for those who crossed them. Like the Chinese dragons, they were water deities. They always lived in lakes and, because of their association with lightning, which is most in evidence at the time of the spring rains, they were believed to control the fertility of vegetation. But, like water, they were capricious and had their good and bad aspects. As the summer showers they were the emblems of fruitfulness, but as the overwhelming rains and floods they were feared, and placated by offerings. Investigations have shown that many of the 'monster lakes' (though not, apparently, Loch Ness) contain offerings, or 'dragon's hoards'.

They are also almost always spoken of as having something growing from the tops of their heads – a horn, or a pair of horns, or a jewel. It is tempting to think that there may be a connection between this and the golden crest of the classical dragon, the horn on the head of Tiamat, the crown of the Naga-king, the trailing feeler-like horns of the early Chinese dragons and even the crowns on the heads of the dragon in the Book of Revelation. People who speak of having seen monsters in the American and Canadian lakes (and also in Scottish and Scandinavian lakes) often mention something on the head – a horn, a protruberance – either on the crown or down towards the neck.

This horn, or jewel, was regarded by the Indians as highly valuable, probably because, like the horn of the equally dangerous rhinoceros, it was extremely difficult to lay hands on. Daniel Brinton says:

> The latter [the Cherokees] related that once upon a time among the glens of their mountains dwelt the prince of rattlesnakes. Obedient subjects guarded his palace, and on his head glittered in place of a crown a gem of marvellous magic virtues. Many warriors and magicians tried to get possession of this precious talisman, but were destroyed by the poisoned fangs of its defenders. Finally, one more inventive than the rest hit upon the bright idea of encasing himself in leather, and by this device marched unharmed through the hissing and snapping court, tore off the shining jewel, and bore it in triumph to his nation.

He goes on to say that:

> The charm which the Creeks presented their young men when they set out on the war path was of very similar character. It was composed of the bones of the panther and the horn of the fabulous horned snake. According to a legend taken down by an unimpeachable authority towards the close of the last century the great snake dwelt in the waters; the old people went to the brink and sang the sacred songs. The monster rose to the surface. The sages recommenced the mystic chants. He rose a little out of the water. Again they repeated the songs. This time he showed his horns and they cut one off. Still a fourth time did they sing, and as he rose to listen cut off the remaining horn. A fragment of these in the 'war physic' protected from inimical arrows and gave success in the conflict.

Since snakes are literally deaf, and dragons are traditionally deaf, the monster, if it responded at all, must have responded to the vibrations produced by the chant.

Just as the Loch Ness monster is the most famous unidentified swimming object in Britain, so Ogopogo of Lake Okanagan in British Columbia is the most famous Canadian edition and Slimey Slim of Lake Payette in Idaho, the best-known American one. But, if there are any lake monsters at all, then there are far more than these three. In his book *In*

Above *This stone lintel (AD 681), from the Maya ceremonial centre of Menche (Yaxchilan) in Mexico, shows a worshipper kneeling before a double-headed serpent deity. The serpent stands on the right wearing an elaborate plumed head-dress, indicating that he is a priest of Kukulcan (plumed serpent), the great god of the Mayas, who was later merged with the Aztec Quetzalcoatl.*

Above *The Loch Ness monster, like the monsters of the American lakes, is rarely seen and no clear photograph has yet been taken. The existence of all these creatures remains in doubt yet has by no means been discounted.*

Search of Lake Monsters, Peter Costello lists well-documented American sightings in California (Lake Folsom), Minnesota (Great Sandy Lake), Montana (Flathead Lake), Nevada (the Alkali Lake), Nevada (Lake Walker), New York (Lake Monona), Oregon (Hollow Block Lake), Utah (Panguitch Lake, Bear Lake and Salt Lake), Vermont (Lake Champlain), Wisconsin (Madison Four Lakes, Lake Waubay, Red Cedar Lake, Lake Pawaukee and Elkhart Lake) and Alaska (Lake Iliamna). Canadian sightings have been recorded in British Columbia (Lakes Shuswap, Cowichan and Pohengamok as well as Okanagan), Manitoba (in a group of connected lakes made up of Sinnipegosis, Manitoba and Dauphin), Ontario (Lake Simcoe), Quebec (Mocking Lake) and Toronto (Lake Duchere).

This list only covers lakes where sightings have been made by two or more people, possibly backed up by Indian legend, and where the witnesses seem to be reliable and have given detailed descriptions and perhaps drawn sketches. Were the list to include every lake covered by Indian tradition, or every lake carrying a single report of something unusual, then none of the large lakes would be omitted. In the same way, many Irish lakes are, or were, reputed to be the home of something large and unknown, and several Scottish Lochs have their 'water horses'. Swedish, Norwegian and Icelandic lakes have the same traditions and some of these traditions make a connection between sea monsters and fresh water monsters, suggesting either that they are related or that some of the lakes are accessible from the sea by way of underground waterways.

Large lakes which are exceedingly cold in their depths and much warmer toward their surfaces, particularly in summer, are subject to strange currents. It is more than likely that some of the witnesses, who described great swirls of water where they believed a huge creature must have risen to the surface and then abruptly submerged, actually saw the brief meeting of two opposing currents. Other sightings may have been of floating logs, large otters or mats of rotting vegetation which give off sufficient gases to propel themselves along in a trail of bubbles. But some of the descriptions do strongly suggest a large creature, often swimming against the current with an undulating movement, sometimes raising its head to look around. And for all the sightings which must be cast aside

Right *A sixteenth-century woodcut showing a sea-serpent coming out of a cave to attack a vessel. In the early days of travel, even the sight of a whale or octopus would have been cause for wonder and amazement. The word 'dragon' was often used to describe any unfamiliar monster, and no doubt the size of the creatures was exaggerated.*

Left *The Temple of the Warriors at Chichen Itza in Mexico includes a pillar in the form of a feathered serpent, with a rattlesnake's tail, which formerly supported the lintel of the temple entrance. In the background is the Pyramid of Kukulcan crowned by the temple dedicated to the sky-god.*

because they refer to logs, otters and so on, it is worth considering that there may have been other sightings which were never reported because the witnesses mistakenly believed that they were seeing logs or otters.

A number of people who have investigated the phenomena of lake monsters, scientists among them, have come to believe quite strongly in their existence. And the fact that none have ever been caught is not much of a mystery. Loch Ness, which has been investigated thoroughly, proved to be immensely deep and cold with appalling visibility at depth. Divers were unable to stay down for long, and the mini-submarine that was used at one stage found visibility so limited that any shy creature, however large, could easily have kept well away from it. And evidence suggests that, if the creatures exist, they are shy. They rarely approach boats or people ashore, and there are numerous frustrating stories of monsters submerging quickly, apparently frightened by the sudden movement of a photographer.

Legends and early writings say that 'remains', supposedly of lake monsters, have been found at the edges of lakes but never, in recent years, a complete and authenticated carcass. Sometimes these remains are said to have been too rotted and incomplete for analysis, although that would not be convincing today, when scientists can build a model of an entire creature on the basis of a single bone. Occasionally a carcass has been examined and found to be a hoax. And there are a few stories of a complete carcass being spotted on a lonely shore and then disappearing before anyone has managed to study or even photograph it. These stories are as common in China as in North America. In China the explanation for the creature's disappearance is usually that it rose to heaven on a cloud from which vantage point it caused a tremendous rain-storm. The obvious possibility here is that the heavy rains revived the creature so that it was able to slip back into the water, or even that the rains washed it bodily back underwater. But it is not usual to find the remains of known aquatic creatures on the shores of inland waters as the kind of storm that would cause such an appearance is rare. Therefore even if all the stories of unusual carcasses were proved to be false, the possibility that there are lake monsters would still exist.

Peter Costello, talking of the creature of Alkali Lake in Nevada, complains that reasonable reports all too easily acquire a veneer of 'American folklore', so that the credible becomes incredible. He says:

> This Lake is a few miles south of Hay Springs. In 1939 the indigent scholars and writers employed on the Federal Writers Project, which was collecting 'American Folklore', summarised the history of the monster there, which they facetiously call Giganticus Brutervicus. When the monster appears the earth trembles and the

Right In Longfellow's tale of Hiawatha, Nokomis, his grandmother, incites him to go and kill a magician called The Pearl Feather, who had wronged her, and who is:
'Guarded by his fiery serpents,
Guarded by the black pitch water,
you can see his fiery serpents,
The Kenabeek, the great serpents,
coiling, playing in the water.'
Hiawatha kills the Kenabeek in order to reach the magician.

skies cloud over. When he comes ashore, to devour calves it is said, a thick mist covers the shore around him. His gnashing teeth rumble like claps of thunder . . .
How reminiscent is this of the Chinese dragons, originally gods controlling the rains and thunder. Did the Chinese coolies working on the American railroads in the 1870s leave one of their deities behind them in Nebraska?

Above *A page from Théodor du Bry's* America *(1584), which describes the Spanish arrival in America to discover that the native Indians live on dragons. One can be seen roasting in the background, while the Spanish gaze in amazement at the dragons tied to a hut.*

The creatures may have been shy, but they have also frequently been described as dangerous. For instance, Iroquois legend tells of a horned serpent who rose from a lake and preyed on the people until it was quelled by a god. This may in fact suggest that the lake inundated the surrounding land from time to time and that the anger, or at least the unreasonable behaviour, of the *genus locii* of the lake was offered as an explanation.

Reports of lake monsters are now rarely noted. This could quite simply be because there are no such things. Possibly earlier sightings were nothing more than misunderstood natural phenomena of one kind or another, which were elaborated by superstitious minds into evidence of a monster. But on the other hand fewer sightings could mean something entirely different. No one who believes in these lake dragons suggests that there was only one nearly immortal creature to each lake. There must always have been a breeding colony, and it is possible that the animals have been so disturbed by the ever-increasing density of boating traffic on their lakes that they now rarely, if ever, breed or, in some cases, they or their food have been polluted out of existence.

Dragons in Alchemy and Psychology

Above *'Because that they of the Quintessence dothe hold Much more precious shall they be than gold.'*
The words, from an alchemical treatise, around this flask show that the purpose of the alchemist was not just to make gold for personal wealth, but to find the panacea, the quintessence, the fifth and highest essence, present in all things, but distinct from the four elements. The green dragon signifies the raw prima materia.

It is possible that the alchemists understood more about the arcane meaning of the dragon than most, in that they accepted his contradictory nature. Being concerned with transmutation, they did not demand stability of form. The dragon was the familiar of the alchemists and they saw him as capable of representing simultaneously each and all of the apparently contradictory aspects of a trinity. The old alchemical texts say: 'The dragon slays itself, weds itself, impregnates itself,' sometimes expressed philosophically as a cycle of 'exist, destroy, create'. The alchemical dragon was often expressed as the Ouroboros, the circular serpent-dragon which bites its own tail, a symbol of unity and of the *prima materia* of the universe which is far older than alchemy and which may have had its origins in Egypt as Apophis, the encircler of the earth.

The alchemists have been seen in various lights throughout their long history. Just as the alchemists were to contribute to later chemistry, so they themselves were preceded, at any rate in Hellenistic Egypt, by artisans concerned to fake the colouring of fabric and metal in order to produce imitation jewels and gold. They were craftsmen, dyers and metallurgists, and it is probable that deceit was rarely intended – just as paste jewellery in a gilt setting may be produced now without serious intent to deceive. But from this work grew the belief that it was possible to transmute base metal into true gold by following formulae based upon contemporary philosophical theories, and so alchemy was born.

In the West, the fourteenth century is often described as 'the age of alchemy', but this was simply a stage in the development of a science whose origins were much earlier. E. J. Holmyard, one-time chairman of the Society for the Study of Alchemy, and author of a general book on the subject, says:

> It appears ... that one of the earliest historical mentions of alchemy is to be found in a Chinese imperial edict issued in 144 BC, which enacted that coiners and those who made counterfeit gold should be punished by public execution .... The fact that alchemy had to be prohibited by law indicates that it must have had a fairly lengthy previous history, and Chinese sources aver that it was first practised by a notability named Tsou Yen who flourished in the fourth century BC.

Holmyard also mentions 'a book on alchemical matters (which) was written in Egypt by Bolos Democritus at a date that cannot be more precisely fixed than as about 200 BC.' And adds, 'Whether the honour should go to China, or whether Egypt established a slight lead, there is no uncertainty about the fact that the main line of development of alchemy began in Hellenistic Egypt, and particularly in Alexandria ....'

There are great similarities between Eastern and Western alchemy, but the connection is not yet clear. Although the outward and practical form of alchemy was always seen as the attempt to make gold, the emphasis in China was upon the attainment of immortality, while in the West it was upon the acquisition of riches. The Chinese saw gold as an imperishable substance and therefore as something which might hold the secret of preventing or reversing the death and corruption of the body. The Westerners tended to see gold simply as wealth. The Chinese sought primarily for the elixir of life, the Westerners for the 'philosopher's stone' – usually understood to be a piece of alchemically manufactured gold which, when mixed with any base metal, would 'grow' more gold, in the same way that a seed planted in base earth will grow an entire plant.

In AD 292 when 'gold-making' was flourishing in Egypt, the Emperor Diocletian decreed that all alchemists were to be banished and their books banned. It is likely that some of the banished alchemists fled eastward in the wake of the Nestorian Christians, and finally arrived at the Persian school of alchemy at Jundishapur, in the fifth century AD. Here they undoubtedly found sympathizers. From the beginning of the ninth century, Mohammedan scholars were particularly concerned with the subject and by the twelfth century were beginning to introduce it to the Christians, especially in Spain where Latin translations of Arabic books gradually became available. In this way alchemy reached Western Europe where it became an immensely popular subject and where, inevitably, it began to attract charlatans who claimed to have made gold, demanded large sums of money to enable them to repeat their experiments (because apparatus and materials were genuinely expensive) and then vanished, with the money. By the eighteenth century, alchemy had declined altogether and given way to an early form of modern chemistry.

However, medieval alchemy should not be seen as having been a total waste of time because it fostered education in the world of matter, and its

Below The green dragon, or raw matter, is overcome and fixed by an antithetical pair: knights Sol (gold) and Luna (silver). They are said to be brother and sister without whom the green dragon cannot germinate and become the philosopher's stone, which is depicted in a variety of images as their son, flanked by the sun and moon. This delicate balance of opposites in one form occurs in the chinese yin/yang, often symbolized by the pearl.

adepts came to understand much about metals and chemical reactions. Francis Bacon said: 'Alchemy may be compared to the man who told his sons that he had left them gold buried somewhere in his vineyard; where they by digging found no gold; but, by turning up the mold about the roots of the vines, procured a plentiful vintage.'

The alchemical writings which are still extant are fragmentary. K.A.J. Hopkins, in *Alchemy, Child of Greek Philosophy*, says:

> From the beginning of alchemy, on through the thousand years of the Dark Ages, Europe and the Near East were so racked with wars, invasions and counter-invasions that not one of the political units has survived. During this never-ending riot, monasteries where the ancient literature was conserved were destroyed and many most valuable writings, records of former attainments, were forever lost to the world. Under these conditions, the survival of an obscure literature, such as that of alchemy, must be considered remarkable .... Since alchemy dealt with one of the least of the mechanical arts, there would seem to be no reason why the writings on alchemy should have been protected or have seemed of value to the monks. It was also the wish of the alchemist to preserve a masonic secrecy in regard to his methods and technique and for this purpose he adopted a blind and misleading language which appears now so repellant to the reader that he is tempted to declare the whole subject a deceit and the literature of no account. It is surprising, therefore, that the pious monks of the old days, with their minds filled with the importance of things of the spirit, should have retained in their collections books seemingly so foreign to their interests. Yet they not only retained them but studied them, as we know from the frequent annotations, interpolations and glosses which have crept into the literature. This interest may perhaps be accounted for by the theoretical side of alchemy which involved a philosophy common to both alchemy and religion, with frequent references to the body and the spirit of the metals.

This 'theoretical side' to alchemy will be dealt with later, but it seems only fair to say at this stage that there was good reason behind the 'masonic secrecy' and the 'blind and misleading language'. During much of its early history the practice of alchemy was illegal, sometimes punishable by death. Therefore the work had to be carried on under cover and essential notes written in a code which would be understood only by other adepts. Even when the art was no longer illegal it was extremely dangerous to be the possessor of alchemical lore. It was not uncommon for an adept to be murdered by one of his fellow alchemists in the hope that the means of creating gold or the elixir of life might be discovered among his possessions.

Thomas Charnock, an alchemist born *c.* 1524, left various writings in which he explains how difficult it was to observe this necessary secrecy, since he, like others of his trade, had to employ craftsmen to make the necessary apparatus. This apparatus would be unlike anything else the craftsman had ever made, and would often be designed by the alchemist himself. Naturally the craftsman would be interested to know what he was making and why, and Charnock gives some of the ingenious explanations he offered to the carpenters, glassblowers and others.

From this need for secrecy sprang the use of symbolic pictures in alchemical texts. Frank Sherwood Taylor, at one time Director of the Science Museum in London, says in *The Alchemists*:

> The figure of the serpent or dragon is the first symbol we meet
> with, and it represents matter in its imperfect unregenerate state.
> The dragon has to be slain, which means that the metals which are
> the subject of alchemy have to be reduced to a non-metallic
> condition and rendered susceptible of receiving a new spirit.

These symbolic pictures and texts would have appeared, to the uninitiated, to be complete nonsense. For instance, here is a small part of a late Greek alchemical poem quoted by Holmyard:

> A dragon springs therefrom which, when exposed
> In horse's excrement for twenty days,
> Devours his tail till nought thereof remains.
> This dragon, whom they Ouroboros (Tail-biter) call,
> Is white in looks and spotted in his skin...
> A monster scorching all the earth with fire,
> With all his might and panoply displayed,
> He swims and comes unto a place within
> The currents of the Nile; his gleaming skin
> And all the bands which girdle him around
> Are bright as gold and shine with points of light.
> This dragon seize and slay with skilful art
> Within the sea, and wield with speed thy knife
> With double edges hot and moist, and then
> His carcass having cleft in twain, lift out
> The gall and bear away its blackened form,
> All heavy with the weight of earthly bile;

Below *Alchemists said that they could not work without the help of God. They believed that there was a spirit hidden in the* prima materia, *and this was eventually interpreted as the Holy Ghost. Here the* prima materia *as the dragon is being fertilized by the Holy Ghost (the* avis Hermetis*).*

69

Above *The three manifestations of the Anthropos during his transformation: body, soul and spirit, from the alchemical treatise* The Ripley Scrowle *(fifteenth century).*

Right *The* prima materia, *shown as the tail-biting dragon, discharges the 'negredo' which has to be skimmed off. This is the first stage in the alchemical process, necessary in the work to achieve the philosopher's stone.*

This poem reads like a picturesque description of a purely mythical situation, certainly not as practical instructions for creating silver, an early stage in gold-making. But, as Holmyard says,

This is not by any means one of the most recondite of symbolic instructions and can indeed be interpreted fairly easily. The dragon was an alloy of copper and silver made by warming the two metals with mercury ['the sea'] in a vessel of fermenting horse dung – a favourite alchemical source of gentle heat. At the end of twenty days no traces of silver and copper remained visible, so that the dragon had bitten its tail until nothing was left. The speckled white copper-silver amalgam was then heated in an Egyptian retort ['comes into a place within the currents of the Nile'] until all the mercury had distilled away and was condensed. The liquid mercury was then poured into a receiver ... and the hot liquid alloy was left in the retort, covered with a black dross of oxide. This 'earthly bile' was then removed and the bright flash of the melted metal underneath could be seen.

Although the term 'dragon' might stand for different things at different stages of the work, (for instance, several dragons fighting indicated that matter was in a state of *putrefactio*, understood to be either the separating out of the elements or else psychic disintegration; a dragon with wings signified the volatile element; a wingless dragon signified the fixed element, and so on), he was generally identified with the metal mercury, or quicksilver. The *Aurelia Occulta Philosophorum partes duo* describes Mercury, the dragon, in terms which embrace all his contradictions at once, as well as hinting at his alchemical properties:

> By the philosophers I am named Mercurius; my spouse is the (philosophic) gold; I am the old dragon found everywhere on the globe of the earth, father and mother, young and old, very strong and very weak, death and resurrection, visible and invisible, hard and soft; I descend into the earth and ascend to the heavens, I am the highest and the lowest, the lightest and the heaviest; often the order of nature is reversed in me, as regards colour, number, weight and measure; I contain the light of nature; I am dark and light; I come forth from heaven and earth; I am known and yet do not exist at all; by virtue of the sun's rays all colours shine in me, and all metals.

Mercurius was called the 'father of all metals' and its ability to change from liquid to solid form, and to effect change in other metals, caused it to be used as a principal ingredient in the efforts towards transmutation. But Mercurius is understood in another way as well – not only is he the father of all metals, he is also the ultimate goal, which is the philosopher's stone, and he is the method of making the stone from the primitive metal. As well as the trinity of create, exist, destroy, he is the trinity of beginning, continuing and completing the work. He is something which must be trapped and mortified in order to be transmuted. Charnock wrote:

> This is the philosophers dragon which eateth up his own taile
> Being famished in a doungell of glas and all for my prevail
> Many yeres I kept this dragon in prison strounge
> Before I could mortify him, I thought it lounge
> Yet at the lengthe by God's grace yff ye beleve my worde
> I vanquished him with a fyrie sword.

Of this sword C.G. Jung, in his *Alchemical Studies*, says: 'In alchemical literature, the procedure of transfixing or cutting up with the sword takes the special form of dividing the philosophical egg. It, too, is divided with the sword, ie. broken down into the four natures or elements.' Just as, in alchemy, the metal is always broken down before any attempt is made to

Above *The* prima materia, *represented in alchemy by the dragon, can be found always and everywhere. The English alchemist, Sir George Ripley (1415–90), declared that* prima materia *was water – the material principle of all bodies.*

build it up into something new. 'As an arcanum, the egg is a synonym for water. It is also a synonym for the dragon .... Mercurius complains that he is "sore tormented with a fiery sword" and yet he is that sword.'

So the slaying of the dragon in alchemical terms is only different to the slaying of the dragon in the terms of epic or legend in that it is a prelude and not an end. The alchemical dragon can be seen to guard the hoard of gold, in the sense that the gold could only be released on his death but after death, after the slaying, came transmutation. The dragon, in a new form, was ongoing, whereas the dragon of heroic legend was simply dead.

Of that other famous symbol of Mercury, the caduceus, or staff around which two serpents twine themselves, J.E. Cirlot in his *Dictionary of Symbols* says:

> The symmetrical placing of two serpents, as in the caduceus of Mercury, is indicative of an equilibrium of forces, of the counterbalancing of the cowed serpent (or sublimated power) by the untamed serpent, so representing good balanced by evil, health by sickness. As Jung has shrewdly observed, this much-used image is an adumbration of homeopathy – a cure effected by what caused the ailment. The serpent therefore becomes the source of the healing of the wound caused by the serpent.

Despite the language and symbolism, much of alchemy can be seen to be concerned with chemical experiments, but there is another side, the 'theoretical' or mystical side. Some say that the mystical side was always

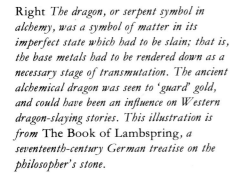

Right *The dragon, or serpent symbol in alchemy, was a symbol of matter in its imperfect state which had to be slain; that is, the base metals had to be rendered down as a necessary stage of transmutation. The ancient alchemical dragon was seen to 'guard' gold, and could have been an influence on Western dragon-slaying stories. This illustration is from* The Book of Lambspring, *a seventeenth-century German treatise on the philosopher's stone.*

the more important and that the 'great work' of the alchemists should always be understood to be concerned with the transformation of base man into pure man. They suggest that many of the writings were talking about this kind of transformation rather than about the transmutation of metals, and that those alchemists who unquestionably conducted painstaking experiments, which were often repeated hundreds of times, were using the physical work as a spiritual exercise. Certainly it required the kind of patience and precision which would make it ideal for the purpose.

Not all alchemists were mystics, but some certainly were, and this interpretation of their work came from various sources. For one thing, because the language of their texts was symbolic it was assumed that the idea of transmutation itself was also symbolic. Many texts refer to Mercury as a spirit. A. J. Hopkins says that the word 'spirit' was intended to mean 'sublimates or substances reduced to the finest sub-division, by which, with the fine material of a dye, metals could be coloured'. But later interpreters, and especially the monks, understood the word 'spirit' in the theological sense. All accounts of the physical process itself indicate that it was redolent with symbolism. The chemical processes of alchemy are such that a base metal can be seen to melt down into a corrupt and blackened mass and then to solidify again as a purer and more beautiful metal, and this is why alchemy was associated with the phoenix, with death and resurrection, either in a literal and chemical way as the death and resurrection of the metal; or by analogy as the death and resurrection of the human body (or the soul) which could be seen to go through the first two stages.

In his *Alchemical Studies*, Jung takes the inner nature of alchemy even further, saying: 'I had long been aware that alchemy is not only the mother of chemistry, but is also the forerunner of our modern psychology of the unconscious.' And later: 'What to the chemist seem to be the absurd fantasies of alchemy can be recognised by the psychologist without too much difficulty as psychic material contaminated with chemical substances. This material stems from the collective unconscious and is therefore identical with fantasy products that can still be found today among both sick and healthy people who have never heard of alchemy.' Jung believed that we were always intended to understand such things from the alchemical writings, saying: '. . . alchemy, as the earliest Greek and Chinese texts show, originally formed part of gnostic philosophical speculations which also included a detailed knowledge of the techniques of the goldsmith and the ironsmith, the faker of precious stones, the druggist and apothecary.'

When Jung describes Mercurius he is speaking not of the metal but of the archetype of Mercury, or Hermes. In Greek or Roman mythology, Hermes or Mercury is the messenger of the gods, with winged heels and helmet, the god of roads and travel and information. In astrology, Mercury is all of these things and also the spirit of restless change which prevents a situation or a personality from being static. To the alchemists the symbolism of Mercury was not essentially different. He was still the spirit of change, of transmutation, still the god of the road from base matter to alchemical gold. The dragon, too, is the spirit of change and therefore the connection between Mercury and dragon is a strong and logical one. Further, in early astrology and early alchemy there is a strong connection between Mercury and Saturn. In fact, some of the early alchemists regarded lead, ruled by the planet Saturn, as the *prima materia*, rather than the quicksilver ruled by the planet Mercury. It is also important to remember that astrologers have always called Saturn 'the greater malefic' (Mars being the lesser) and both Saturn and Mercury, although not evil, do have connections with the devil.

Here, then, in the practical and in the psychological interpretations of the dragon are all the associations known to belong to him: he is chaos, the primeval chaos that must be overcome by the hero figure; he is water; he is the spirit of change; he has diabolic connections.

However, this dragon is not evil. He has in him all possibilities, both good and evil, while being in a sense morally neutral. It is suggested that the dragon's head can be identified with the Christ and the tail with the anti-Christ. The *Theatrum Chemicum Britannicum* (1652) says: 'The whole body obeys the head, and the head hates the body, and slays it, beginning from the tail, gnawing it with its teeth, until the whole body enters into the head and remains there forever.'

The practical alchemists speak of the 'slaying of the dragon', the basic material, as a necessary stage in transmutation. Speaking in psychological terms Jung describes it in much the same way:

> The dragon, or serpent, represents the initial stage of unconsciousness, for this animal loves, as the alchemists say, to dwell in caverns and dark places. Unconsciousness has to be sacrificed; only then can one find the entrance into the head, and the way to conscious knowledge and understanding. Once again the universal struggle of the hero with the dragon is enacted, and each time at its victorious conclusion the sun rises, consciousness dawns, and it is perceived that the transformation process is taking place inside the temple, that is, in the head.

In *Man and His Symbols*, a collection of essays edited by Jung, Joseph L. Henderson says that the battle between hero and dragon shows:

Right *The flask containing the three-headed dragon was, like all the imagery of alchemy, both practical and symbolic. It was egg-shaped, and from it the philosopher's stone should hatch. The colours of the heads would have indicated, to an adept, the correct sequence of processes.*

the archetypal theme of the ego's triumph over regressive trends. For most people the dark or negative side of the personality remains unconscious. The hero, on the contrary, must realise that the shadow exists and that he can draw strength from it. He must come to terms with its destructive powers if he is to become sufficiently terrible to overcome the dragon – i.e. before the ego can triumph, it must master and assimilate the shadow.

In regarding the dragon as a principle rather than as a creature, the mystical alchemists and the psychologists seem to have seen him as a force operating beneath the consciousness of man, which must be brought forth into consciousness. The Chinese saw the dragon principle as a force operating beneath the surface of the earth itself, which emerged, and was encouraged to emerge, at the correct time to bring energy to the world. The dragon is the fertilizing, regenerative principle, the creature of spring, which lies dormant until the time comes for it to rise and flow forth. In the *I Ching*, the first hexagram is known as the Dragon Hexagram – it is *Ch'ien*, the Creative.

The Chinese did not see this fertilizing principle as a random thing but as a cosmic breath which flowed in specific currents, just as the blood flows along the veins of the body. Chinese geomancy (*feng shui*) has been defined by Chatley in *Encyclopaedia Sinica* as 'the art of adapting the residences of the living and the dead so as to co-operate and harmonise with the local currents of the cosmic breath'.

In *The View Over Atlantis*, John Michell suggests that the art was practised in other countries too, most notably in Britain and western France. He talks of 'leys', a name coined by Alfred Watkins who first discovered a system of ancient straight tracks all over Britain and who viewed these, more prosaically, as old traders' routes. Michell believes that these leys are *lung-mei*, or dragon paths, which follow the line of dragon power and which are marked by stones, mounds, hill notches and churches. He says:

> When visiting some of these mounds, stones and ancient church sites associated with the dragon, it is hard to avoid the impression that they were located according to principles similar to those adopted by the geomancers of China. There it was said that the dragon's heart is to be found at a lonely knoll standing in a small plain or valley among the hills. From the central spot the veins of the dragon current run over the surrounding ridges. Near the heart its force, pent in by the hills, is strong and active. At this centre the dragon and the tiger, the male and female currents, meet harmoniously.

It is certainly true that a great many sites associated with the dragon consist of some kind of hill or mound rising out of the surrounding landscape. The fact that most of these are now topped by a church or chapel indicates that they were probably sites of ancient sanctity. And, to complete the circle, many are associated with Saints George, Michael or Martha, all well known for their dragon-slaying activities.

The three apparently different dragons can be seen to be so closely related that one leads to another in a kind of circle in which all points are virtually the same. The alchemists' dragon, the principle of dynamic change which must die to create, leads to the psychologists' dragon, the unrealized unconscious with its potential for being overcome and enlightened, which in turn leads to the geomancers' dragon, latent fertilizing energy waiting to grow and to be reaped.

Which brings us back to the Ouroboros. Jung says that the eternal cycle of birth and death was 'represented in ancient alchemy by the symbol of the ouroboros, the dragon that bites its own tail. Self-devouring is the same as self-destruction, but the union of the dragon's tail and mouth was also thought of as self-fertilisation. Hence the text says: "The dragon slays itself, weds itself, impregnates itself".'

Above *The alchemists continually reiterated that the 'opus' (work) proceeds from the one and leads back to the one, that is in a circle, expressed by the dragon biting its own tail.*

Here, the Mercurial dragon, or serpent, *devours itself in water or fire; as dragon, it devours itself, and as dragon dies to rise again as the lapis or philosopher's stone (From 'Elementa chemicae', 1718).*

Dragons on Maps

Below *A detail from a copy of the Genoese World Map of 1457. The map is a portolano, or pilot's chart, drawn on sheepskin. Portolanos generally gave very precise details of coastal features and less precise details of inland territories. However, this particular one is unusual because it differs from contemporary coastal charts sufficiently to suggest that its author may not have been a professional cartographer. It is generally endowed with animals and people and the dragon is placed, as he so often was, in the Ethiopian region.*

Map-making developed gradually. The earliest known maps were little more than crude notes or diagrams made of relatively short journeys. All that was required of them was that they should show the way there and back again and nothing was depicted that did not actually impinge on the route. Gradually the uses of maps extended, and people required not only simple route maps but also military maps, world maps and maps to indicate the boundaries of lands. In their early forms, these world maps often give an indication of a particular culture's view of cosmology – the known world sometimes being shown to be completely surrounded by water, supported on the backs of elephants, flat and supported on four turtles in a river, and so on. Possibly the oldest world map still in existence is a clay tablet dated about 3800 BC and showing part of Northern

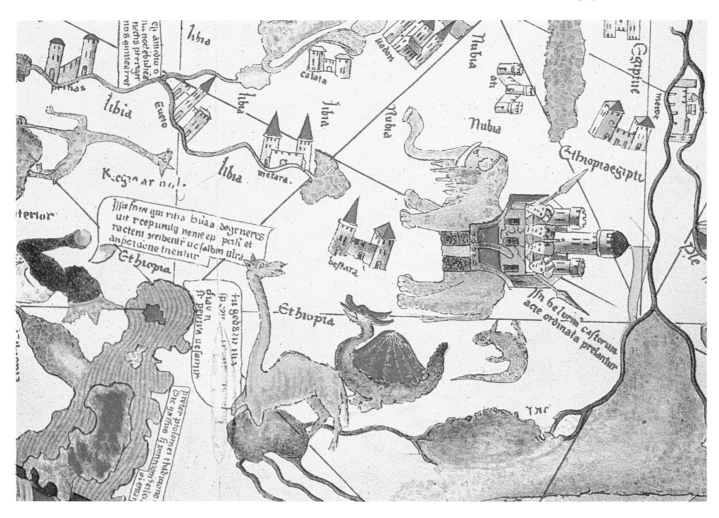

78

Mesopotamia; and the British Museum has in its possession a Babylonian clay tablet, *c.* 500 BC, which shows a circular universe with Babylon at its centre, the whole surrounded by a kind of cosmic ocean, which was regarded as something of a threat.

Few really ancient maps survive. From those which do it is possible to see that Babylonian and early classical maps were the work of philosophers and Egyptian maps the work of surveyors, who have also left plans of buildings and the map of the Nubian gold mines. Not until Ptolemy, who was working in Alexandria in the second century AD, were the principles of map making laid down, roughly as we know them now, and there is still controversy about whether or not Ptolemy himself ever drew maps.

'Here Be Dragons' was a statement which appeared on a few post-Ptolemaic maps, sometimes accompanied by drawings of dragons, apparently to indicate areas of unexplored wilderness. It appears almost always at the boundaries of the mapped region and, in terms of what they are intending to convey, the words have a faintly biblical ring to them; Here Be Dragons; Here Be Desolation. The idea that the known world is surrounded by desolation is an ancient one, and is still true today, except that our desolation takes the form not of an encircling ocean but of space. But before the Bible linked the dragon with lost and empty places and set it to howl in the wilderness, early creation myths were describing a huge serpent, called Apophis by the Egyptians, who bound the earth with his body. Being a form of dragon, the conflict between good and evil was strong in him, and while he held the earth together, preventing it from flying into little pieces as it spun through space, he also longed to break his

Above One of a series of illustrations from a medieval collection of travellers' tales, the Livre des Merveilles, *which included those of Marco Polo. This one was supposedly inspired by Marco Polo's quite accurate description of an alligator, and shows how good reporting could be turned into fantasy — especially important in an age in which pictures carried more weight than words.*

bonds and destroy it. It may be that the idea of the encircling serpent was so deeply rooted that it was believed that if you travelled dangerously far beyond the known boundaries you would reach the edge, and encounter the awful dragon himself.

The Ebstorf World Map is one of the earliest specifically to include dragons among its fauna, but then it also includes pictures of numerous flying snakes, a dog-like creature breathing fire and Noah in his ark. It was drawn *c.* 1215, probably by a teacher of Canon Law called Gervase of Tilbury, who at one time served the Guelphs as a provost in Ebstorf. The map was discovered in 1830 in a Benedictine monastery in Ebstorf where it had been used by the monks as an altar-piece. It was moved to Hanover where it was destroyed in World War II, but facsimiles remain. Like so many early ecclesiastical maps it gave information other than purely geographical, and the same applies to the Hereford World Map, which is still on view at Hereford Cathedral. Information for maps of this kind, with a strongly religious significance, is likely to have come from the Bestiaries. Like the Bestiaries, the maps were teaching aids, with the emphasis on morality and the symbolic significance of the creatures rather than on scientific accuracy. Although the physical existence of dragons was almost certainly held to be true, their distribution would not have been of major importance to those who saw the maps, since dragons were always placed elsewhere. The maps were on view in Western Europe and the dragons were comfortingly remote – usually in Africa or India (two countries which were often confused at this time).

By the later Middle Ages cartographers were producing quite detailed maps upon which information was not limited to coastal outlines, the situation of mountains and the courses of rivers, but included towns, people and animals. In 1546, Pierre Desceliers produced the first of his highly respected world maps. Desceliers had advanced far beyond religious allegory and, although its faults and omissions are evident today, his map was probably as nearly scientifically accurate as the limitations of the time would permit. Yet on it, as well as such creatures as llamas, alligators, snakes, monkeys and armadillos there is, unquestionably, a dragon.

Even sophisticated world maps such as this were decorative, and it has been suggested, not least by Dean Swift, that drawings of animals were used merely to fill in the blanks in the cartographer's geographical knowledge.

> So Geographers in Afric maps
> With savage pictures fill their Gaps;
> And o'er uninhabitable Downs
> Place Elephants for Want of Towns.

But Wilma George, in *Animals on Maps*, refutes this, pointing out that it is quite likely that, in certain areas, there *were* elephants in place of towns. And, having completed a serious study of the distribution of animals on antique maps, she comes to the conclusion that the majority of them were correctly placed, with the possible exception of camels. Of course, it may well be that the domestic pack-bearing camel then covered greater distances than we now realize. Wilma George discovered that in many cases a particular animal actually had a wider range than the early cartographers allowed it and that, therefore, their sins were more often of omission. Writing of the Desceliers' map in particular, she says that all the animals are more or less accurately portrayed and in their right places. And that those, like the dragon, which are questionable, do not appear on later maps, which seems to indicate that the cartographer realized he had misinterpreted early written descriptions of the creatures and so had deliberately omitted them in later editions. But what is especially interesting is that dragons are so often shown in the company of animals which are well-observed and recognizable, allowing for a few mistakes which are hardly fundamental, such as elephants with tusks protruding from almost all parts of their heads and mouths but the right ones, and rheas with four legs.

It is not hard to see why mythical beasts should appear among the strange creatures on the Ebstorf and Hereford maps, but maps such as the one by Desceliers have every appearance of precision. Why, having taken the trouble to depict the right animals in the right places, should he suddenly incorporate a fabulous monster? And if, which seems unlikely, he was merely using his representations of animals to fill in the spaces, there was still no need to resort to myth, there were plenty of real animals available, many of them quite as extraordinary as any dragon. The answer seems to be that people wanted to believe in dragons.

Information for these later maps came from travellers of all types – explorers, merchant sailors, pilgrims and even armies. The quality of the reports that were fed to cartographers was variable in the extreme, and those who received them were clearly in no position to judge of their truth. In *Allegory and the Migration of Symbols*, Rudolf Wittkower says:

> ... the reports by travellers, though finally decisive in revolutionising our conception of the inhabited world, did not further the advance of natural science, ethnology and geography in a straight line. They were almost without exception a curious mixture of solid observation and fabulous tradition. These men, from the Dominican and Franciscan monks of the 13th century to Columbus and Fernao de Magellan (late 15th century) went out to distant countries with a preconceived idea of what they would find.

What is more, those who received the information seem to have had a preconceived idea of what they would hear so that they listened, and believed, selectively. To quote Wittkower again:

> Sir John Mandeville left a long narrative of a journey to Africa and Asia in the middle of the 14th century which, as is now well known, never took place. His report is one long story of marvels and fabulous tales, and it seems characteristic of the disposition of the human mind that it was this work which had the greatest success of all descriptions of travels. It circulated in beautifully illuminated manuscripts and from the end of the 15th century onwards appeared in all languages and in innumerable editions, decorated with a vast number of woodcuts.

Sir John Mandeville on the subject of dragons sounds even less scientific than the Bestiaries, and although he sometimes admits that his report is hearsay it was apparently taken for truth in some quarters.

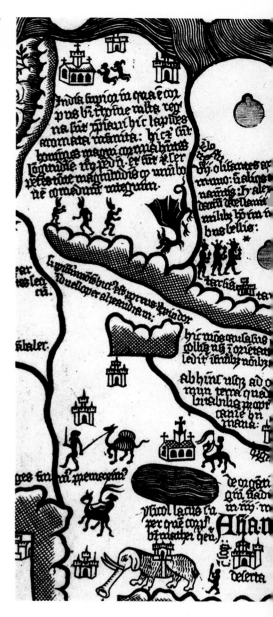

Above *A detail from the Borgia World Map of 1435. The map is engraved on iron and is thought to have been designed as a wall decoration. The dragon at the top is only one of several which appear, together with fairly accurate representations of camels, horses, and elephants. It is anonymous and acquired its name because it was bought from an antique shop by Cardinal Borgia for his museum.*

... some say that in the Isle of Lango is Ipocras, in the Manner of a Dragon, who is an hundred foot long, as men say, for I have not seen her, and they of the Isles call her the Lady of the Country, and she lyeth in an old Castle, and showeth herself thrice in the year, and she doth no man harm, and she is thus changed from a Damsel to a Dragon, through a Goddess that men call Diana; and some say that she shall dwell so unto the time that a Knight come that is so hardy as to go to her and kiss her mouth; and then she shall turn again to her own kind, and be a woman, and after that she shall not live long. And it is not long since a Knight of the Rhodes, that was hardy and valiant, saith that he would kiss her, and when the Dragon began to lift up her head against him, and he saw she was so hideous, he fled away, and the Dragon in her anger bare the Knight to a Rock, and from thence cast him into the Sea.

Various meanings can be read into the story. It is Diana, the goddess of chastity, who has turned the maiden into a dragon, possibly to protect her virginity. The promise is that if a knight kisses her she will be made into a

Right *A graphic interpretation of dragons, indicative of the universe, with the sun, moon, and Earth at the centre. The illustration forms the frontispiece from* Astronomicum Lasareum.

MO. GUMAR.

woman (a euphemism, perhaps). And if he does make her into a woman he must, of course, marry her. Later in the story Mandeville makes it clear that marriage with her was the Knight's prize. But perhaps virginity defended for too many years goes a bit stale and, when he gets a good look at her, the knight cannot bring himself to take her.

However fantastic the story, and however much it can now be seen to have been based on some kind of allegory, it was read as a truth from a far and strange land where anything could happen. That there were marvels in the East was an ancient tradition, firmly established long before the birth of cartography as we know it. As travellers began to explore these previously mysterious lands, and to report back, they either confirmed the existence of the expected marvels or else moved the marvels to less accessible places – from India and Ethiopia to Abyssinia and South Africa.

It was quite common for the texts of several travellers' reports to be collected together into one illustrated manuscript, and one of the most famous of these 'collectanea' is the Codex 2801 in the Bibliothèque Nationale in Paris which was gathered into one volume at the beginning of the fifteenth century for John the Fearless, Duke of Burgundy. Wittkower says:

> It is worth considering the character of the texts assembled in Codex 2801. The manuscript begins with Marco Polo's book. This is followed by Friar Odoric's fanciful report of his journey which lasted from about 1316 to 1330. Number 3 is the account of William of Boldensale's pilgrimage to Egypt and Palestine in 1336. No. 4 consists of the letters of the Great Khan to Pope Benedict XII, in 1338, and the Pope's answer. Next follows the report on the states of the Great Khan, written by John of Cor, Bishop of Sultaniyah; then John Mandeville's imaginary travels, the Armenian Hayton's *Historia orientalis*, and finally the Florentine Ricoldo di Montecorvo's description of his eastern journey, begun in 1288. Thus most of the texts are travellers' reports presenting a colourful mixture of the East, ranging from reliable historical, topographical and ethnographical material to pure flights of fancy.

Above *A detail of a map of Abyssinia by Ludolfi in Allardt's* Atlas Major *of 1683. It shows a single-horned rhinoceros but typically African elephants with large ears. The dragon is an exaggerated* Draco volans, *or flying lizard, which has wrapped its tail around the legs of the elephant.*

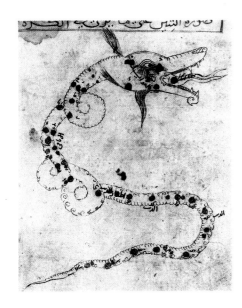

Above *Celestial maps, such as this miniature, were designed at a time when astronomy and astrology were closely connected. In the casting of horoscopes, the constellation of Draco indicates the area of highest potential with its head, and the area of greatest opposition with its tail (from* The Book of Fixed Stars, *by 'Abd al-Rahman al-Sufi, Iran, late fourteenth century).*

... the illustrations of Codex 2801 can teach us an important fact: the cycle of illustrations binds together the various texts, so different in value and veracity if judged by modern standards. The uninterrupted sequence of these illustrations, similar in tenor from beginning to end, makes it evident that for the contemporary reader all these texts were on the same level of reality.

Readers of this manuscript still lived largely in a pictorial age and the pictures would have carried more weight than the text. This, coupled with the idea that anything can happen in foreign parts, made the dragon-images that appeared throughout completely acceptable.

Of all the authors collected in the Codex, Marco Polo was by far the most reliable. He was a Venetian traveller of the second half of the thirteenth century, best known for his descriptions of the court of Kublai Khan. He was a careful observer who began his travels when he was only 17 and possibly before he had had time to gather too many preconceived ideas of what he might find. The veracity of much of Marco Polo's reporting is in little doubt today, but the later illustrator of his writings seems to have been affected more by conventional expectations of monstrous men and beasts than by Marco Polo's words. In fact, in a sense the pictures did not really illustrate the text, they presented a separate, though related, view of reality. For instance, Marco Polo's description of a Chinese alligator, although colourful and vivid, was largely accurate. He called it a huge serpent or reptile with two short legs near the head, jaws wide enough to swallow a man and huge sharp teeth. The omission of the two back legs is in many ways a minor error, they are not evident when the alligator lies in the water, and the long body ending in the heavy, flat, propelling tail is serpentine. Marco Polo made no mention of wings, or a serpent's head on the end of the tail, or of other dragonish attributes, but the artist supplied all of these.

It is important to remember that just as conventional thought today dismisses the idea of the dragon as pure fairy-tale, conventional thought in the Middle Ages was quite as rigid in its acceptance of the dragon as reality. That, coupled with the dragon's regular appearance in the text or pictures of travellers' tales may be how most, although not all, dragons got on to maps. However, few animals were depicted to scale, all were generally drawn much the same size as each other. One of the best examples of a Draco-type dragon appears at the foot of a map of Abyssinia drawn by Ludolfi and published in 1683 in Allardt's *Atlas Major*. In later maps, such as this one, dragons had generally withdrawn to the cartouche or the decorative border, but they were still in the company of known animals and in the regions where they were supposed to abound.

Dragons appeared not only on maps but also on terrestrial globes, which began to be produced around the mid-fifteenth century. The construction of the terrestrial globe was regarded as highly as the construction of a world map.

Globes were usually made in pairs, one terrestrial and one celestial, and the image of the dragon, as the constellation Draco, was always present, curling across the top of every celestial globe, just as he overshadowed every astrolabe. Celestial globes were based on the observations of astronomers which were more accurate than the observations of travellers upon which terrestrial maps and globes were based. For a long time astronomy and astrology were closely interconnected, and while certain astrolabes were designed to aid navigation and astronomical studies, others were built to facilitate the casting of quick horoscopes. These astrolabes had independently moving arms, each of which represented a planet. Lying right across each one was the figure of the dragon, used to determine the position of the Moon's nodes (that is, the point at which the lunar orbit intersects the earth's orbit) known as the Head and Tail of the Dragon. The Head pointed to the area of life where the subject of the horoscope could expect highest achievement and the Tail to the area of greatest opposition.

Here, within the discipline of astronomy and, to a certain extent, astrology, the dragon is less problematic. He does exist, as a constellation, just as the crab, the scorpion and the hunter exist. But to the first astronomers who observed the particular configuration of stars that is called Draco, he was not solely of the sky but was born in, or reflected, an earthly myth. He was actually Ladon, the guardian-dragon who protected the Tree of Golden Apples in the Garden of the Hesperides and who was flung into the sky when he was killed by Heracles.

It is impossible to say whether the earthly dragon came first, and was elevated to the stars to explain the outline of a constellation, or whether the dragon-like constellation itself inspired the stories of earthly dragons. Certainly the earliest dragon stories were generated at a time when men were far more aware of the sky than we have been in recent history. But whether the dragon rose to, or fell from, the stars, the saying of the philosopher-astrologers is still relevant to him, 'As above, so below'.

Left *One of a pair of globes – this one celestial – made by Jacob and Arnold van Langeren in 1589.*

85

Dragons in Zoology

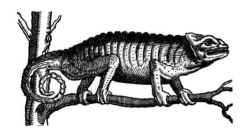

Above A page from The Historie of Foure-Footed Beastes' *(1658) by the seventeenth-century naturalist Edward Topsell. The appearance of the dragon in a natural history book, next to a fairly realistic chameleon (top), shows the extent of belief in dragons at the time, and its inclusion in the book would also have fostered this belief.*

Most dragon stories fall into one of three categories. There are the fairy-tales, featuring a purely fabulous beast who was occasionally lovable, like Puff the Magic Dragon, but more often terrible, like Tolkien's Smaug; allegories in which the dragon stood either for man's baser instincts or for the devil himself, like the dragon slain by St George, or else for harsh meteorological conditions, like the dragons responsible for flood and tempests; and there are the stories from travellers, or students of the natural sciences, who present the dragon as a zoological reality, as actual as the elephant or cobra.

Those writers who give the dragon a place in zoology fall into two groups. There are those who believe that it is a distinct species, rarely seen only because it lives in inaccessible areas and is dying out. Into this group come those whose work influenced the early cartographers. And there are those who explain it away in terms of known creatures, extant or extinct. Into this second group come most of the modern writers who have touched on the subject.

One of the most persuasive of the writers whose belief in dragons was literal was Edward Topsell who, in the middle of the seventeenth century, wrote *The Historie of Serpents: or The Second Book of Living Creatures* (the first being his *Historie of Foure-Footed Beastes*); *Wherein is contained their Divine, Natural and Moral Descriptions, with their lively Figures, Names, Conditions, Kindes and Natures of all Venomous Beasts: with their several Poisons and Antidotes; their deep hatred to Mankinde and the wonderful work of God in their Creation, and Destruction.* His section on dragons begins: 'Among all kindes of Serpents, there is none comparable to the Dragon, or that affordeth and yeeldeth so much plentiful matter in Historie for the ample discovery of the nature thereof . . . .'

He mentions the fact that dragons have excellent, he says 'vigilant', eyesight, and goes on to say 'and therefore it is faigned that they had the custody not only of the Golden Fleece, but also of many other treasures. And among other things Alciatus hath an emblem of their vigilancy standing by an unmarried Virgin'. (This is a reference to the *Emblamata cum commentaris* of Andrea Alciatus, a humanist who died in 1550, and the emblem in question shows Minerva, or Athene, in full armour with a dragon at her side. The accompanying note or commentary suggests that the dragon is chosen as the consort of the goddess because 'the safeguard of all things belongs to this, Wherefore his house in Groves and sacred Temples Unmarried Maids of guards must never miss, Which watchful are to void loves snares and net'. This idea of the dragon as the guardian of virginity is continued in the convention of calling a chaperone a dragon and raises an interesting question about the motives of St George.)

However, this is the 'moral description' of the dragon. His 'natural' description is very detailed and accompanied by sketches. Speaking initially of Western dragons, Topsell says: 'Their mouth (especially of the most tameable dragons) is but little, not much bigger than a pipe, through which they draw in their breath, for they wound not with their mouth, but with their tales only, beating with them when they are angry. But the Indian, Aethiopian and Phrygian dragons have very wide mouths, through which they often swallow in whole fowls and beasts.' On the subject of the Indian dragons he is very precise. He says that there are two kinds, a marsh and a mountain dragon. 'Their snouts are very strong, resembling the great ravening fishes; they have beards of yellow-golden colour, being full of bristles: and the Mountain-dragons commonly have more deep eye-lids than the Dragons of the Fens. Their aspect is very fierce and grim, and whensoever they move upon the earth, their eyes give a sound from their eye-lids, much like unto the tinkling of Brasse, and sometimes they boldly enter into the Sea and take Fishes.' His description of the dragon sounds like the creature of the Bestiaries.

Towards the end of the nineteenth century there was a tremendous upsurge of interest in psychical and physical phenomena. In *The Dawn of Magic*, Louis Pauwels and Jacques Bergier suggest that towards the end of the nineteenth century Western civilization was busily closing its doors and its ears to new ideas, a trend which, they say, was not reversed until the century ended. In 1875 the Director of the American Patent Office resigned, grumbling that he was obsolete because there was nothing left to invent, and Helbronner, who became the greatest European authority on physical chemistry and made remarkable discoveries, was told by his tutor, Professor Lippmann, that he would be wise to steer clear of the subject since it was all sewn up. It is almost as though the upsurge of interest in primitive and extraordinary animals was a result of this attitude: impossible to go on further, so why not use the energy to discover wonders in the past or, perhaps, in the imagination. Several books on fabulous beasts were published around this time. Dragons appeared in most of them and, quite frequently, were treated seriously by writers

Left Another page from Topsell's natural history, showing one type of dragon and its similarity to the serpent.

concerned to brush away what they saw as prejudice and to present a reasonable case for the existence of the beast. For instance, in 1886 Charles Gould wrote in the Introduction to his *Mythical Monsters*:

> For me the major part of these creatures are not chimeras but objects of rational study. The dragon, in place of being a creature evolved out of the imagination of Aryan man by the contemplation of lightning flashing through the caverns which he tenanted, as is held by some mythologists, is an animal which once lived and dragged its ponderous coils, and perhaps flew; which devastated herds, and on occasions swallowed their shepherd; which, establishing its lair in some cavern overlooking the fertile plain, spread terror and destruction around, and, protected from assault by dread or superstitious feeling, may even have been subsidised by the terror-stricken peasantry who, failing the power to destroy it, may have preferred tethering offerings of cattle adjacent to its cavern to having it come down to seek supplies from amongst their midst.

And later, in the body of the book, he makes it clear that he believes that legend and myth only followed fact:

> Again, believing as I do in the existence of some great undescribed inhabitant of the ocean depths, the much-derided sea-serpent, whose home seems to be especially adjacent to Norway, I recognise this monster as originating the myths of the Midgard Serpent which the Norse Elder Edda have collected, this being the contrary view to that taken by mythologists who invert the derivation, and suppose the stories current among the Norwegian fishermen to be modified versions of this important element of Norse mythology.

And later still, in 1906, John Vinycomb wrote in *Fictitious and Symbolic Creatures in Art*:

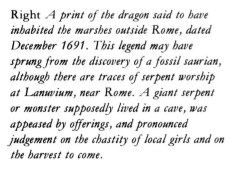

Right *A print of the dragon said to have inhabited the marshes outside Rome, dated December 1691. This legend may have sprung from the discovery of a fossil saurian, although there are traces of serpent worship at Lanuvium, near Rome. A giant serpent or monster supposedly lived in a cave, was appeased by offerings, and pronounced judgement on the chastity of local girls and on the harvest to come.*

Drago come uiueua il primo di Decembre 1691 nelle paludi fuori di Roma.

It is often argued that the monsters of tradition are but the personifications of ... violent phenomena of nature, and so, no doubt, they are, and have been; but the strange fact remains that the same draconic form with slight modifications constantly appears as the type of the thing most dreaded .... Looking at the widespread belief in dragons, there seems little doubt that the semi-myth of today is the traditional successor of a once really existent animal ....

To people who would say that the dragon is too extraordinary a creature ever to have lived, Charles Gould points out that nobody believed Madame Merian when she described a bird-eating spider or Victor Hugo when he described a devil-fish (giant cuttlefish) but that both were vindicated by later discoveries. And he also suggests that the dragon may have been badly observed and not always clearly described. Certainly the more extraordinary and the more unexpected a sight, the more likely it is to be misinterpreted because, not knowing what he is looking at, the observer doesn't know what to look for. And so the Mexican Indians, seeing Pizarro and his horsemen, assumed man and horse to be one beast, a kind of centaur.

The hints from Vinycomb, Gould and the others point towards the dinosaurs, whose fossilized remains have made their appearance at various stages throughout the history of man; and in fact in *Sacred and Legendary Art*, Anna Jameson says:

At Aix a huge fossilised head of one of the Sauri was for a long time presented as the head of the identical dragon subdued by St Martha; and St Jerome relates that he himself beheld at Tyre the bones of the sea monster to which Andromeda had been exposed.

It was not so much bad observation as misinterpretation that figured in quite recent reconstructions based on the finding of just such fossil bones. Herbert Wendt, in *Before the Deluge*, says:

The discovery of the [fossilized remains of the] Iguanadon inspired a spate of highly imaginative saurian reconstructions. Mantell wrote his popular *The Wonders of Science* and wanted a picture of an Iguanadon for the frontispiece. The artist John Martin obliged with such a portrait, which turned out to be that of a short-legged dragon with a massive tail. When the famous Crystal Palace Exposition opened, its garden was adorned with sculptures of gigantic antediluvian creatures. Waterhouse Hawkins the sculptor had also represented the Iguanadon as a clumsy four-footed dragon. Fifty years were to pass before the world learned that the animal did not walk on all fours but erect on two legs, and that it fed peacefully on the shoots of coniferous trees.

Earlier reconstructions were far more bizarre; the cyclops, for instance. The cyclops was said to be an enormous giant with a single eye in the centre of his forehead, and Herbert Wendt points out that: 'An elephant skull with its remarkable nasal opening, looking deceptively like two merged eye sockets, might cause an uninstructed observer to believe in the existence of gigantic one-eyed creatures.' In the same way, quantities of large bear bones found in caves in Central Europe may have given rise to dragon legends and to the names and stories attached to caves such as the Drachenfels in the Siebengebirge where Siegfried slew the dragon of the Nibelung Saga.

Huge bones were also found in China, and in quite considerable numbers to judge from the amount of very precise recipes for their use in medicine which have been collected by historians. The 'dragon bones', if gathered at the right time, in the right way and by the right people (those collected by women had no value whatsoever), ground and mixed with herbs, and then correctly administered, were seen as cures for most known ills. Quantities of fossil bones must have been swallowed by generations of Chinese.

Nevertheless, it seems more likely that the bones lent their weight to an already existing idea than that they inspired it. Even if one or two complete skeletons of dinosaurs may have turned up, as proof of the one-time presence of something almost unbelievably huge and certainly reptilian, this kind of discovery would have been rare, and at a time when communications were extremely limited. Most of the finds would have consisted of sections only, hinting at size but not at structure, and it is hard to believe that dry bones alone could have been the seed of an idea that was to become so robust. Herbert Wendt says:

> The occasional finding of a fossil saurian may here and there have led to the birth of a dragon legend. Some scientists trace our ideas of dragons back to primitive man's encounter with giant snakes, crocodiles and other large reptiles. Others suggest that the cave bear gave rise to the legend. Nevertheless, the dragon of fairy-tales bears no relation to giant snakes, crocodiles, cave bears, or other living or dead creatures; on the contrary, the dragon of our imagination does indeed resemble a giant saurian. We do not know why that is so, for it is incontestable that man never saw the giant saurians.

It does appear to be true that man as we know him did not exist during the Age of the Reptiles, but a remote ancestor of man did exist then, just as the descendants of the dinosaurs are now thought still to be with us, in the form of the birds. In *The Dragons of Eden*, Dr Carl Sagan says:

> The most recent dinosaur fossil is dated at about sixty million years ago. The family of man (but not the genus *Homo*) is some tens of millions of years old. Could there have been man-like creatures who actually encountered *Tyrannosaurus Rex*? Could there have been dinosaurs that escaped the extinctions in the late Cretaceous period? Could the pervasive dreams and common fears of 'monsters', which children develop shortly after they are able to talk, be evolutionary vestiges of quite adaptive – baboon-like – responses to dragons and owls?

Without question, dragonish reptiles once preyed on mammals and Dr Sagan suggests that this conflict, which continued for thousands of years, is reflected in the continuing enmity between man and dragon that is described in Western mythology. Although it does not account for the

Eastern attitude towards dragons, the argument is a compelling one, particularly if it is accepted that dim and distant race memories of such creatures are a possibility. But there are other theories, which take the dragon from the area of, strictly speaking, palaeontology, into the area of zoology. Of creatures still in existence, there are five major contenders for the title – one of which is highly controversial.

The controversial beast is the ubiquitous lake monster of North America, Canada, Britain and Scandinavia. It has many of the attributes of the dragon in that it haunts lakes and inspires legends about the need to propitiate it with sacrifice and it is associated with weather phenomena, but it is rarely seen and there are as yet no pictures of it which are acceptable to everyone. The possibility remains that one day a lake monster will be caught, or at least photographed, and that it will turn out to be, quite obviously, a dragon. But so far it is only a possibility and, some would say, a slim one.

Another possibility is the crocodile or alligator. There are obvious points in its favour. It is unquestionably reptilian; it is dangerous enough to inspire fear and legends offering calamities; it is likely to eat anyone venturing too close. Its tail is strong and dangerous. What is more, it is traditionally said of dragons that they are so hot by nature that they gape for air to refresh them. Jeremiah XIV, 6, says: 'Wild asses did stand in the high places, they snuffed up the wind like dragons.' And basking Nile crocodiles lie on the banks of rivers with their jaws gaping so widely and for so long that the small birds called the Egyptian Plover (*Pluvianus aegyptius*) hop in and out of their mouths, picking their teeth or pecking leeches from their throats. The crocodiles tolerate this intimate form of

Below *A sight like this could easily have led to tales of multi-headed monsters, with claws, and scaly bodies, which eat anything (including humans) that comes too near. These American crocodiles were photographed in the Everglades National Park.*

feeding for the comfort it brings them. Herodotus, Pliny, Solinus and others correctly described this form of mouth-valeting of the Nile crocodile but nevertheless the sight is open to misinterpretation. And this possibility of misinterpretation is another point in favour of the crocodile being the prototype of the dragon.

De Natura Animalum, a Greek work of the mid-third century AD, describes the dragon in terms which clearly suggest a crocodile or alligator, saying:

> The Phrygian history also states that dragons are born which reach ten paces in length; which daily in midsummer, at the hour when the forum is full of men in assembly, are wont to proceed from their caverns, and (near the river Rhyndacus) with part of the body on the ground, and the rest erect, with the neck gently stretched out, and gaping mouth, attract birds, either by their inspiration, or by some fascination, and that those which are drawn down by the inhalation of their breath glide down into their stomach – (and that they continue this until sunset), but that after that, concealing themselves, they lay in ambush for the herds returning from the pasture to the stable, and inflict much injury, often killing the herdsmen and gorging themselves with food.

But there are points against the crocodile as well. Despite their penchant for lying in the water with only their eyeballs showing, neither crocodiles nor alligators are difficult to observe. They can be seen when they lie in the shallows and they can be seen when they bask ashore. And a properly observed crocodile does not look like a dragon.

In India the marsh crocodile or mugger (*Crocodylus palustris*) is still venerated in some areas and kept in 'sacred captivity', where its behaviour

Below *A winged dragon from Ulyssis Aldrovandi's* Serpent and Dragon History, *Book II, 1540. This faked composite was to appear later in Edward Topsell's natural history books alongside real animals.*

DRAGO COME SI RITROVA NELLE MANI DELL'
INGEGNIERO CORNELIO MEYER

Left *The skeleton of the same dragon that inhabited the marshes outside Rome, as seen in the possession of Ingegniero Cornelio Meyer. It may have been a fossil, or a faked composite.*

can be readily observed and the differences between it and the dragon duly noted. And the Chinese alligator (*Alligator sinensis*) has co-existed with the dragon in Chinese literature for centuries (although its existence was not accepted by Western zoologists until 1879). Its bones and liver were valued as medicine, but they were listed separately to dragon bones in the same books. What is more, this particular species is quite small, never exceeding one and a half metres (five feet) in length, and it is hardly credible that it should have inspired so great a legend and at the same time remained acknowledged as a separate creature. And finally, the dragon which is most like the alligator is the Western dragon, which is heavy, antagonistic and pitiless, and not the Chinese dragon, which is light and airy. Yet alligators live in China, and neither they nor crocodiles live in Europe.

The next possible dragon-prototype is almost any large snake, but especially the boa constrictor or python. The mythology of the snake has already been shown to be virtually world-wide, and even today it arouses more complex emotions, more fear and revulsion, and also more fascination than any other living creature. Part of its evil reputation is based on the fact that many snakes are dangerous. Those which are not poisonous can kill by winding themselves around a victim and squeezing the life out of him, a peculiarly intimate and horrific way of killing. Any culture touched by Hebrew tradition is also permeated by the attitude of Jehovah towards the serpent of Eden, and by the fact that, after its actions there, mankind and reptiles were apparently set against each other forever by God himself. Even in cultures which venerated and worshipped the snake, it was acknowledged to be capricious, just as dragons tend to be. Its lidless eyes and unwinking stare not only add to its power to fascinate, but give it the reputation for eternal vigilance which is also enjoyed by the

Above *The dramatic leap of the flying* Draco volans *in Indonesia, which, as the name suggests, may well have been a source for dragon stories, even though this flying lizard is very small.*

dragon. Pliny's description of Indian 'dragons' winding themselves around elephants to crush them to death sounds very like a description of a large snake. If it is accepted that the feathered serpent of South America is truly a dragon, then he is half snake, and the word 'worm' or 'snake' or 'serpent' can be seen to be interchangeable with the word 'dragon'.

Possibly the two most dragon-like snakes are the Indian rock python (*Python molurus*) and the African python (*Python sebae*). In his book *The Fascination of Reptiles*, Maurice Richardson says that the maximum length for the Indian rock python is about seven and a half metres (25 feet) and that it is found '. . . outside India, from West Pakistan to South China, and should really be called the Asiatic rock python. It likes water and can stay under it for quite a long time. It eats pigs and small deer, ducks, pheasants and peacocks. Its strength as a constrictor must be very great, for the remains of a leopard were taken from the stomach of an eighteen-foot python, the wounds on whose skin were quite slight'. The python administers a severe bite before winding its coils around its victim, just as the spider, which arouses much the same kind of revulsion, bites its victim before winding it up in silk. Of the African python, which is found throughout most of Africa south of the Sahara, Richardson says: 'This is the python of antiquity, the Serpent of Old Nile', and adds that 'in the wild (it) is naturally quite savage. There is an authenticated record of its having attacked an African woman washing by the banks of a river'.

Since any dramatic incident tends to become exaggerated in the telling, it is not hard to believe that the African python could be credited with bringing down elephants. But although in some of the early creation myths the snake and the dragon blend, and although serpent-worship and dragon-worship are undoubtedly interconnected, the snake is still not,

strictly speaking, a dragon. It is certainly closely related, either mythologically or physically, and it is more than likely that it was the inspiration for some dragon stories, just as the bones of cave bears or dinosaurs were probably the inspiration for others.

However the dragon is so much more than a snake. Its outline and behaviour patterns are generally similar, but the dragon has appendages which no snake ever has, and these are generally the same from country to country across the world; sometimes legs, sometimes wings, a reptilian head on a neck which is distinct from the body in a way in which a snake's is not. The dragon may be in essence an elaborated snake, or the snake may be a simplified dragon, but to cast the snake as the prototype of every dragon is simply not convincing.

The next possibility is *Draco volans*, the small flying lizard. Several pictorial representations of dragons quite obviously do represent the Draco gliding lizard, which is really extremely dragon-like. The Greek historian Herodotus may have been speaking of Draco when he talks about Arabia, and the frankincense that comes from there, saying:

> The Frankincense they procure by means of the gum styrax, which the Greeks get from the Phoenicians. This they burn, and thereby obtain the spice; for the trees which bear the Frankincense are guarded by winged serpents, small in size, and of various colours, whereof vast numbers hang about every tree. They are of the same kind as the serpents which invade Egypt, and there is nothing but the smoke of the styrax which will drive them from the trees.

Above *Perhaps the nearest living creature to a real dragon is the Komodo dragon, a large monitor lizard with many 'dragon' attributes, except that it has no wings. It has a forked tongue, which flicks like dragon-fire; it lays eggs; it can swim; it has a scaly body and can be dangerous if aroused. It is found on a small group of islands in Indonesia, of which Komodo is one.*

Left *In 1978 there was a report in the* London Times *from India of a battle between a village and a huge python, which had half swallowed a man. Both the man and the python died in the struggle, and locals told the tale using the word 'dragon'. There is also an authenticated story of an African python, like the one in the photograph, attacking a woman on a river bank.*

He goes on to mention that the wings of this creature are not feathered but closely resemble those of a bat.

Draco is found now in the Indo-Malayan region where it flies, or rather glides, on bat-like leathery wings, from tree to tree. Stories of its appearance and behaviour could easily have been carried over considerable distances by travellers, so that the idea of it could have reached areas where the lizard itself never lived. However, if these stories were in fact the source of dragon legends they must have been inflated, quite literally, out of all proportion. Draco is a tiny lizard, measuring not much more than 12 centimetres (five or six inches) from nose to tail. It is not poisonous and it could never have posed a threat of any kind to man. Just one picture, if sufficiently widely circulated, could have inspired several different dragon legends, and the lizard is actually called Draco, so its likeness was certainly acknowledged, but it is stretching credulity too far to suggest that this little creature was *the* dragon. As with the snake, if the dragon ever lived then Draco was a relation, even a miniature descendant perhaps, but it seems unlikely that its existence accounts for more than a few out of the whole body of dragonish legends.

And so, at last, to the popular favourite, *Varanus komodoensis*, the Komodo dragon. This is a particularly large monitor lizard whose smaller relatives are found in Africa, tropical Asia, Australia and on islands in the Pacific. The Komodo dragon is found on a small group of Indonesian islands, of which Komodo is one, and although wingless and, according to Dr Sagan, 'not very bright', it is remarkably dragon-like. In common with most other lizards it continues to grow throughout its lifetime (although the rate of growth is not yet established), lives probably for about 50 years, and can attain considerable size. In his book *Zoo Quest for a Dragon*, David Attenborough records that the specimen that he caught on Komodo in 1956 'measured a full twelve feet in length'. Monitors can swim, and their flattened tail indicates that they are semi-aquatic in habit. They lay eggs in true dragon fashion, but they don't cherish their progeny. The eggs are buried, to allow them to incubate, and, when they hatch, the first danger that faces the young dragons is the same as the danger facing young crocodiles – they will be eaten by their parents and elders. It is not certain what the small dragons eat, probably insects, but when adult they are certainly carnivorous, and can bring down their prey with a single blow from their strong tails, just as Edward Topsell and others have described. Although they don't deliberately hunt man, they would certainly be extremely dangerous if antagonized. In 1956 a member of an American expedition unwisely tangled with a Komodo dragon and had to be evacuated by seaplane for emergency hospital treatment. This dragon also has the forked tongue depicted in many dragon pictures, and it has been suggested that this tongue, flickering constantly in and out of the mouth as it does, may have been the root of the stories of dragons breathing fire.

Against the Komodo dragon is the problem of distribution. Its habitat is so remote that it seems unlikely that it could have persuaded virtually the whole world into a belief in its powers. However, other smaller monitor lizards have a wider distribution, and it seems possible either that the smaller monitors were still sufficiently impressive to have excited world-wide awe, or that the Indonesian Islands are the present habitat of a creature which once enjoyed a far wider range.

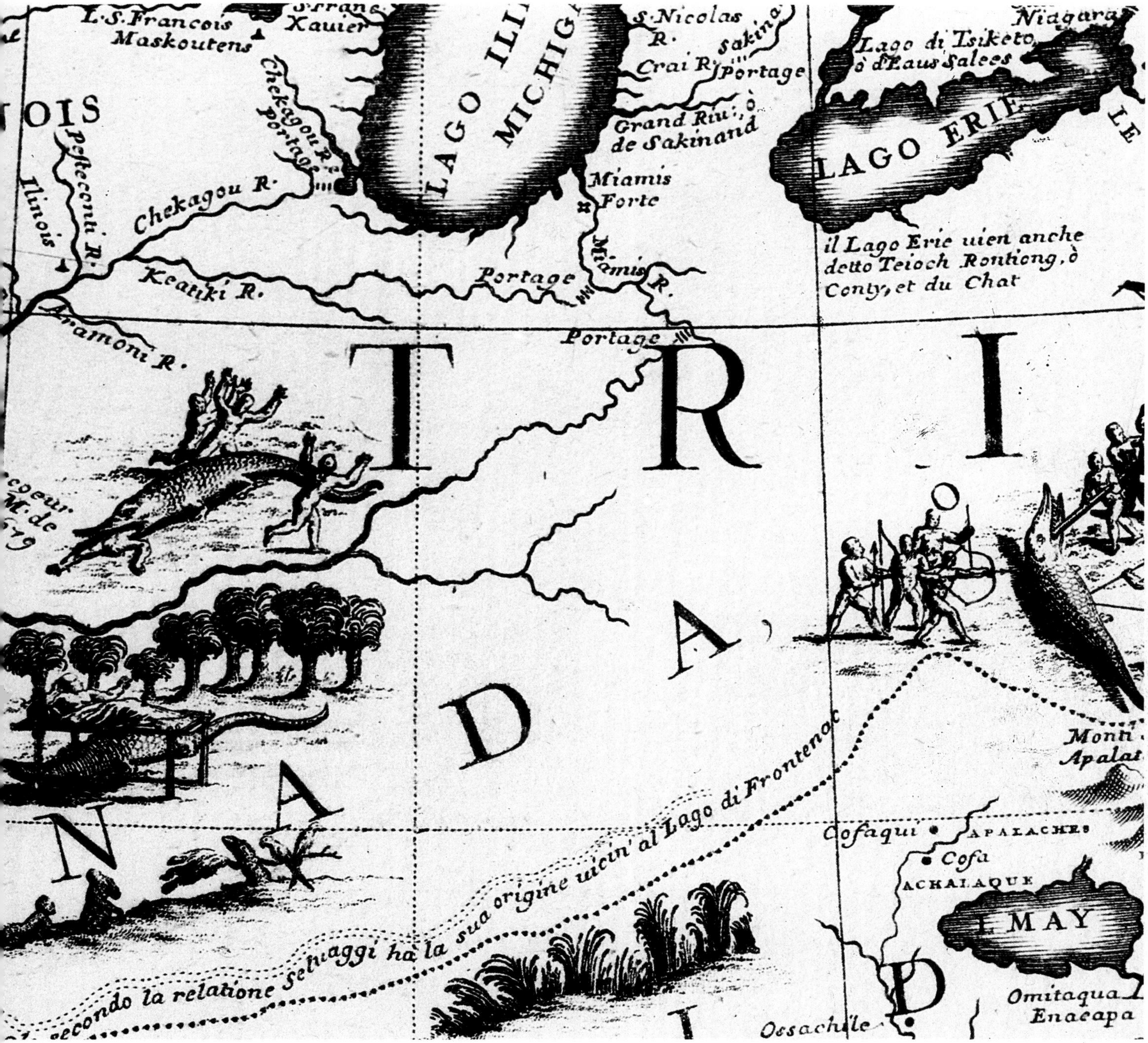
L.S.Francois Maskoutens
Xauier
S.Nicolas R.
Crai R.
Portage
Lago di Tsiketo, ò d'Eaus Salees
Niagara
LAGO ERIE
Grand Riu., de Sakinand
Miamis Forte
Chekagou R.
Keatiki R.
Portage
Miamis R.
il Lago Erie uien anche detto Teioch Rontiong, ò Conty, et du Chat
Portage
T R I
O
A
D
A
N
Monti Apalat
Cofaqui
APALACHES
Cofa
ACHALAQUE
I MAY
Omitaqua
Enacapa
Ossachile
secondo la relatione Selvaggi ha la sua origine uicin' al Lago di Frontenac

However like dragons these various reptiles may be, they are still not dragons. If the idea of the dragon already existed, then a sighting of any of these, in the right circumstances, might serve to confirm it, but no single one of them is truly satisfactory as the originator of the legend. If Dr Sagan's theories are correct, and we dimly remember a time when the world was divided into conflict between the reptiles and the mammals, then any one of these five would once have had the power to reawaken the ancient dread. The power would have diminished as the creatures became better known and even commonplace and the last vestiges of it would linger on in the lakes of North America, Britain and Northern Europe, where the dragon-descendants, the lake monsters, still retain their mystery.

Above A map of America of 1697 shows a crocodile swallowing a man, and another being lanced down the throat in true dragon-slaying style. Images such as these may have influenced dragon-lore. Dragons are often depicted swallowing a man, or spitting him out.

Dragons in Epic and Folklore

While most of the epic dragons are presented as fictitious, some of the legendary dragons were presumed to have existed in scale and blood. And yet it is when you look directly at either kind, in an attempt to discover its origins, that the dragon-image becomes exceptionally elusive. Some of the most famous stories seem to lead back in time to a minor and relatively undramatic beginning. The bones of a cave bear, a storm in a forest, a puritanical attitude to fishing on a Sunday, these seem to be the unpromising seeds. Suddenly, legend is empty of dragons. Yet from these seeds, these dragon eggs, grew creatures that were so robust and well-rounded, so three-dimensional in form and impact, so powerful both as adversaries and as literary themes, that once again the world is as full of dragons as anyone could reasonably hope. A paragraph in Guillaume Figuier's *World Before the Deluge* (1891) follows the thread of a dragon legend back to its beginnings in a Carinthian cave:

> In the city of Klegenfurth, in Carinthia, is a fountain on which is sculptured a monstrous dragon with six feet, and a head armed with a stout horn. According to popular tradition this dragon lived in a cave, whence it issued from time to time to ravage the country. A bold and venturous knight at last kills the monster, paying with his life the forfeit of his rashness. The head of the pretended dragon is preserved in the Hotel de Ville, and this head has furnished the sculptor for a model of the dragon on the fountain. A learned professor of Vienna on a visit to the city recognises it at a glance as the cranium of the fossil rhinoceros. Its discovery in some cave had probably originated the fable of the knight and the dragon – and all similar legends are capable of some such explanation when we trace them back to their sources and reason the circumstances on which they are founded.

This explanation may, in its way, also account for one of the great epic dragons of all time, Fafnir. Fafnir is a creation of the poets of Norse mythology, whose remaining works are all that are left of the traditions and beliefs of the Teutonic race. An enormous amount of material was destroyed by order of the Christian priests, and the sombre philosophy of the Norsemen, with its belief in the inevitable destruction of the gods themselves, comes down to us in *Beowulf* in England, the *Nibelungenlied* and a few other fragments in Germany, and in the two Icelandic *Eddas*. Since the twilight of the gods was a foregone conclusion, there was no salvation to be reached for, so the emphasis is not upon survival but upon heroism. It matters that you kill the dragon, and it matters that you do so with courage. It does not matter that you die in the attempt.

Sigurd is the most famous of the Norse heroes, whose story is told in the Norse *Volsungasaga*. It is much the same as the story of Siegfried, the dragon-slayer of the *Nibelungenlied*, upon which Wagner's *Ring Cycle* is based. The dragon, Fafnir, was once a man who slew his own father for the sake of a hoard of gold and the magic ring which could create more. He assumed the shape of a dragon in which form he guarded the gold, and in which form he was in turn slain by the hero. Stolen dragon-gold was always cursed and Sigurd eventually died, as did Siegfried and, indeed, all the heroes, swept away into the dark on tides of courage. The dragon slain by Siegfried lived and died in the Drachenfels on the Rhine, and the Drachenfels were probably originally named for the huge bones, most likely of cave bears, which were once found there.

The *Nibelungenlied* Saga has a complex plot which it is not necessary to spell out here, but it can be seen as the struggle of one man to find enlightenment, which he then loses in a sleep of forgetfulness, after which disaster follows. The dragon Fafnir can be seen as representing the lower, animal nature of man and it is relevant that when he has killed the dragon and accidentally tasted a drop or two of its blood, Siegfried can understand the language of the birds.

Left *Siegfried slays Fafnir, one of the greatest of the epic dragons. Arthur Rackham's illustration for Wagner's* Siegfried and the Twilight of the Gods.

Another great epic dragon is the one described in *Beowulf*, an Anglo-Saxon poem, the oldest surviving copy of which is a manuscript *c.* 1000, written in 'classical late West Saxon', and housed in the British Museum. The first part of the Saga is taken up with describing Beowulf's battle with the terrible Grendel, and later with Grendel's monstrous mother. And then, when Beowulf has ruled his people, the Geats, wisely for 50 years, the Saga describes the stirring of the dragon:

> Half a century
> he ruled it well: until One began
> – the king had grown grey in the guardianship of the land –
> to put forth his power in the pitch-black night-times
> – the hoard-guarding Dragon of a high barrow
> raised above the moor.
> Men did not know
> of the way underground to it; but one man did enter,
> went right inside, reached the treasure,
> the heathen hoard, and his hand fell
> on a golden goblet. The guardian, however
> if he had been caught sleeping by the cunning of the thief,
> did not conceal this loss. It was not long till the near-
> dwelling people discovered that the dragon was angry.

The slave who disturbed the dragon was a thief on the run from a flogging who got inside the barrow more or less by accident. Once inside, he could not resist stealing the golden treasure cup, part of the hoard of a

Below According to the Norman poet, *Wace, in his chronicle* Roman de Brùt, *King Vortigern built a tower which collapsed. His wizards advised him to slay a man 'born of no earthly father'. They therefore brought Merlin to him, but Merlin explained that under the tower was a pond, and if they emptied the pond they would find two dragons, one red and one white, and they would fight. This proved to be true, and King Vortigern asked Merlin to interpret this event. He replied that it prophesied kings and battles to come.*

dead race, whose sole surviving member had hidden it in the barrow in an earlier age. Indeed, before the slave, the dragon himself found the hoard by chance:

> The Ravager of the night,
> the burner who has sought out barrows from of old,
> then found this hoard of undefended joy.
> The smooth evil dragon swims through the gloom
> enfolded in flame; the folk of that country
> hold him in dread – He is doomed to seek out
> hoards in the ground, and guard for an age there
> the heathen gold: Much good does it do him!

When he discovers that his hoard has been tampered with, the dragon can hardly restrain himself until night-time, when he bursts forth, vomiting flames, and burns all the houses in the vicinity. It is worth noting that here, as in so many other places, the dragon is referred to both as a worm and as a serpent.

Beowulf's own hall is burned down by the dragon, and with a premonition of death the king prepares to take action. With the unfortunate slave as a guide, he sets out and, with the help of his kinsman, Wiglaf, he kills the dragon, but himself dies of wounds and venom.

Although Wiglaf, having helped Beowulf to kill the dragon, takes the gold in his name, it is eventually sacrificed with Beowulf's body. As Michael Alexander says, in his notes to his translation:

the dearly bought gold is to be sacrificed with the body in tribute; the Geats will not profit by it, they will become the boast of the raven. A curse traditionally attaches to buried treasure – whether it applies to Beowulf, the slave, the dragon, the Geats or the 'last survivor's' people who took the gold from the ground is not clear. Beowulf certainly dies, but the possibility that he is damned seems quite excluded.

(This is shown by the line 'Soul left its case, going its way to the glory of the righteous.')

These are the dragons of high drama. The dragons of legend and folklore are rather more domestic and, although ferocious, tend to be more local in their impact and, just occasionally, to inspire humour in their chroniclers.

Britain is particularly rich in 'wormes' and dragons. The best-known are probably the Dragon of Wantley and the Laidley Worm of Lambton. But there are plenty of others, including the Welsh Worme which indirectly gave Denbigh its name (because the conquering hero returned to the town shouting triumphantly 'Dim bych, dim bych!' – 'No dragon, no dragon!'); the Grisely Worme of Lofthouse in Yorkshire; the Sockburne Dragon, which may have been an inundation of the River Tees which half surrounds the village, and about which an early account says: 'Sir John Conyers, knight, slew that monstrous and poysonous vermine or wyverne, which overthrew and devoured many people in flight, for that the sent of that poison was so strong that no person might abyde it.'; the Linton Worm which was slain by William de Somerville whose

Above *The famous Norse dragon-slayer Sigurd, depicted on a carved roundel of a stave church in Hylestad, Norway. The middle and bottom circle show Regin forging and testing the sword, with which Sigurd kills the dragon Fafnir.*

victory is said to have inspired the dragon-slaying sculpture in the porch of the church there, which stone is said once to have borne the inscription:

> The wode Laird of Lariestone
> Slew the wode worm of Wormieston,
> And won all Linton parochine.

The Laidley Worm of Northumberland was different, and reminiscent of the one described by Sir John Mandeville. She was a princess of Bamburgh who was changed into a serpent by her wicked stepmother. Word of the disaster reached her brother overseas and he returned, restored her to her proper shape with a kiss, and turned the stepmother into a toad.

The traditional story of the Laidley Worm of Lambton is told in *English Legends* by Henry Bett:

> The legend of the Lambton Worm is similar to that of the Sockburne Worm, but there is more picturesque detail. The heir of Lambton went fishing in the Wear on Sunday, and hooked a small worm, which he flung into a well. The worm grew into a mighty serpent and, emerging from the 'Worm Well', took up its abode in the Wear, where it used to lie coiled around a crag in the middle of the river. It also frequented the 'Worm Hill', a green mound near the well, where it would coil itself nine times round the hill, leaving traces which lasted until modern times.

(Similar traces are found in other parts of the country, perhaps most notably around Glastonbury Tor. These have been described as mazes, or ceremonial walk-ways to the tops of sacred mounds. A more likely explanation is that they are the furrows left by heavy ploughing, in medieval times or even earlier. The effects of soil and water erosion, aided by gravity, have emphasized these furrows over the years, and so has the fact that sheep, and indeed people, tend to walk to and fro along them, it being easier to weave to and fro up an incline than walk directly ahead.)

> It was now the terror of the country, and levied a daily tribute of nine cows' milk, which was put ready for it at the hill. If this was not forthcoming it devoured man and beast. Meanwhile Lambton had gone on a crusade. On his return he was shocked to see the result of his youthful folly and undertook the task of destroying the worm.

(At first it seems strange that Lambton should have felt himself to be responsible. He only fished up the creature, which eventually made its way back to where he found it. Presumably it would have grown into a ravager of the countryside in any case. They key seems to be that he fished on a Sunday, the implication being that such impiety could only be evil.)

> After several combats, in which he was foiled by the serpent's power of reuniting any parts of its body that were divided, he went to consult a wise woman. By her advice he armed himself in a coat of mail which was studded with razor blades, and then

Above *Thor fishing for the Midgard Serpent, his eternal enemy and the monster that envelops the Earth with his coils and causes terrible sea storms. Though Thor successfully hooked the serpent, the giant Hymir cut the line (Viking bronze plaque, eighth century).*

posted himself on a crag in the river to await the monster's attack. When the worm came it wound itself madly around the knight, who saw the monster cut in pieces by its own fury, while the stream washed away the severed parts of its body and prevented these from joining again. But the witch had promised Lambton the victory on condition that he would slay the first living thing he saw afterwards. Lambton had told his father, when he heard three blasts on the horn, to unleash a favourite greyhound, which would fly to him at the sound, and was meant to be the victim, but on hearing the horn the father was so glad that he forgot, and ran himself to meet his son. In this tragic dilemma young Lambton went again to the wise woman, who prophesied that by way of penalty [for not killing his father], no head of the Lambton family should die in his bed for seven generations, or, according to some accounts, for nine generations.

It is interesting to see the number nine so firmly associated with a British dragon. Nine, which in numerology stands for spiritual achievement, is a number usually strongly associated with the Chinese dragon, who is furnished with nine times nine scales, has nine sons and so on.

The story of the Dragon of Wantley parallels the story of the Lambton Worm quite closely. It is traditionally told in an old English Ballad:

Old stories tell how Hercules
A dragon slew at Lerna,
With seven heads and fourteen eyes,

Left *According to the Apocrypha, Daniel was a friend of Cyrus the Persian. Cyrus worshipped a Babylonian god, Bel, and a great dragon. Daniel refused to worship either, but undertook to slay the dragon without weapons, to prove that it was no god. He boiled a mixture of pitch, hair and fat which the dragon ate, and then burst. The Babylonians, incensed at the death of their god, demanded that Daniel be thrown to the lions, or they would kill the king. The idea of slaying the dragon 'without sword or staff' occurs in the Tiamat myth.*

The story of Daniel is here told on a window in the church of St Etienne (fourteenth century).

To see and well discern-a:
But he had a club, this dragon to drub,
Or he had ne'er done it, I warrant ye:
But More of More-hall, with nothing at all,
He slew the dragon of Wantley.

This dragon had two furious wings,
Each one upon each shoulder;
With a sting in his tail as long as a flail,
Which made him bolder and bolder.
He had long claws, and in his jaws
Four and forty teeth of iron;
With a hide as tough as any buff,
Which did him round environ.

Have you not heard how the Trojan horse
Held seventy men in his belly?
This dragon was not quite so big,
But very near, I'll tell ye;
Devour'd he poor children three,
That could not with him grapple;
And at one sup he ate them up,
As one would eat an apple.

All sorts of cattle this dragon would eat,
Some say he ate up trees,
And that the forests sure he would
Devour up by degrees:
For houses and churches were to him geese and turkies;
He ate all and left none behind,
But some stones, dear Jack, that he could not crack,
Which on the hills you will find.

Hard by a furious knight there dwelt;
Men, women, girls, and boys,
Sighing and sobbing, came to his lodging,
And made a hideous noise.
O save us all, More of More-hall,
Thou peerless knight of these woods;
Do but slay this dragon, who won't leave us a rag on,
We'll give thee all our goods.

This being done, he did engage
To hew the dragon down;
But first he went new armour to
Bespeak at Sheffield town;
With spikes all about, not within but without,
Of steel so sharp and strong,
Both behind and before, arms, legs, and all o'er,
Some five or six inches long.

It is not strength that always wins,
For wit doth strength excel;
Which made our cunning champion
Creep down into a well,
Where he did think this dragon would drink,

And so he did in truth;
And as he stoop'd low, he rose up and cried, boh!
And kick'd him in the mouth.

Oh, quoth the dragon with a deep sigh,
And turn'd six times together,
Sobbing and tearing, cursing and swearing
Out of his throat of leather:
More of More-hall, O thou rascal,
Would I had seen thee never;
With the thing at thy foot thou hast prick'd my throat,
And I'm quite undone for ever.

Murder, murder, the dragon cried,
Alack, alack for grief;
Had you but miss'd that place, you could
Have done me no mischief.
Then his head he shaked, trembled and quaked,
And down he laid and cried;
First on one knee, then on back tumbled he;
So groan'd, and kick'd, and died.

Left *More of More-hall defeating the dragon of Wantley with his ingenious spiked armour.*

The Dragon of Wantley had a certain panache, and it is perhaps a little sad to know that his story has been explained away. The dragon, it appears, was a crooked lawyer of Wantley who, after cheating various people out of money and land, managed to cheat three orphan children out of their rightful inheritance. Their case was taken up by a Mr Moore of More-hall. He fought the 'dragon' in the courts and defeated him, whereupon, it is said, the villain died of rage. The satirical ballad which was written about these events eventually began to be believed as literal truth and the Dragon of Wantley not only became a legend, but probably inspired other legends too.

Some other dragons are as easy to demolish as the Dragon of Wantley, or at any rate, from the point of view of physical reality. In his book on serpents, Topsell tells a dragon legend:

> The Chroniclers of the affairs of Chius do write, that in a certain valley near to the foot of the Mountain Pellenaus, was a valley full of straight tall trees, wherein was bred a dragon of wonderful magnitude or greatnesse, whose only voice or hissing, did terrifie all the inhabitants of Chius, and therefore there was no man that durst come nigh unto him, to consider or to take a perfect view of his quantity, suspecting only his greatnesse by the loudnesse of his voyce, until at length they knew him better by a singular accident worthy of eternal memory. For it happened on a time that such a violent winde did arise, as did beat together all the Trees in the Wood, by which violent collision the branches fell to be on fire, and so all the wood was burned suddenly, compassing in the Dragon, whereby he had no means to escape alive, and so the trees fell down upon him and burned him. Afterward, when the fire had made the place bare of wood, the inhabitants might see the quantity of the Dragon, for they found divers of his bones and his head, which were of such unusual greatnesse, as did sufficiently confirm them in their former opinion: and thus by divine miracle was this monster consumed, whom never any man durst behold being alive, and the Inhabitants of the Countrey safely delivered from their just conceived fear.

It may not be too much to suggest that the 'voice or hissing' of the dragon was actually the wind in the trees. It is stated clearly that no one saw the dragon alive. Bones were found later, but they were 'divers bones', which sounds as though they were many and scattered, and not a complete skeleton. Many creatures must have died in the fire, scattering their bones, and as the people expected to find the remains of a large creature, it is possible that the bones of several large animals were presumed to be the bones of only one. It could, of course, be argued that the people were probably hunters and could be expected to recognize the bones of their regular prey. There are two possible answers. One is that there might well have been large creatures who lived in the wood and never left it, and who therefore would never have been seen or hunted by the people, who never entered it – the ubiquitous cave bears, for instance. The other is that in the course of a forest fire, which would cause trees to crash down, fossilized saurian bones might have been uncovered. This seems particularly likely in the case of the head.

The bones of a cave bear, the inadvisability of fishing on a Sunday, a

Right The King Bahram Gur *loved hunting, and according to* The Book of Kings *(1435), he spied a dragon that resembled a male lion, with a mane, and women's breasts. With his bow and arrow he shot the dragon through the head and chest. With his dagger he then split open the dragon's body and found a young man dead and congealed in blood and venom inside.*

satirical ballad, a high wind; it doesn't seem difficult to explain away dragons, whether correctly or not. This does not destroy the literary or emotional impact of great epic poems like *Beowulf*, but it does threaten to take all the magic and mystery out of the image of the dragon himself, to explain him away in terms of other things. But it is important to remember how strong this image of the dragon was that it should spring so readily to mind, either as a metaphor for a wicked man or as an explanation of a natural phenomenon. It is easy to say, now, that a particular dragon was only a wind howling in a forest. But it is important to remember that, once, people hearing the howling decided that what they heard was a dragon, not a lion or a wounded elephant, not even a chimera or a giant.

Stories of loathsome scaly animals, however they may be exaggerated, must originally spring from something, and perhaps not all can be brushed aside so easily as those above. There is a particularly interesting section in the story of the Linton Worm, as told by James, the Eleventh Lord of Somerville, in his family history of the Somervilles which was written about 1679. The section begins when William de Somerville has just arrived at Jedburgh, by chance, and hears tell of the Worme: 'The people who had fled ther for shelter, told soe many lies, at first, that it increased every day, and was beginning to get wings: others pretended to have seen it in the night, and asserted it was full of fyre, and in tyme, would throw it out, & c, with a thousand other ridiculous stories.' The passage goes on to describe how Somerville goes and looks at the dragon. There is no description of what he sees, apart from a note that the dragon creeps out of its den and rears up to look back at him. Somerville concludes that, as he suspected, it is not as dangerous as all that. He goes away and prepares a specially long, iron-plated, spear with a contraption half-way up that will hold lighted peat. He trains his horse to overcome its fear of fire, and when he is ready he charges the dragon and kills it by thrusting the burning spear down its throat.

Because of that passage, this rather minor dragon legend has quite a different impact. Somehow, down the years, comes an image of a real animal, which was elaborated out of all recognition by fearful people, but which was then viewed dispassionately by a soldier, seen not to be so fearsome after all, and despatched in the usual manner. It is the very fact that the Eleventh Lord does not subscribe to all the exaggeration that gives the story a ring of truth.

Right *It may be significant that this Victorian print of the May Day festival includes a dragon. It was probably part of the ritual to celebrate the new spring, rebirth and fertility, just as the Chinese use the dragon for their New Year festival.*

Dragons in Art and Heraldry

Just as he appears in most mythologies, the dragon also appears in most art forms, where he has puzzled generations of art historians. It may be worth considering that the concept of 'interpretation', when applied to artistic representations, can work in two ways. The more obvious way is from the idea to the expression of it; the artist having taken a known myth or legend and interpreted it in the form which suits his style and the age in which he worked. But in the case of very early works of art, ancient religious icons, for instance, or the Sumerian cylinder seals, the interpretations which are available to us now have more often flowed in the other direction, from picture to idea. And, when much of the record of a religious or philosophic belief is pictorial, the possibility of misinterpretation is always present.

In the notes to his *The Greek Myths*, Robert Graves has reinterpreted some familiar stories, for instance, the judgement of Paris. The accepted interpretation of an early icon showing a shepherd boy apparently handing an apple to one of three beautiful women standing before him, is that the shepherd, Paris, was forced to judge which of the three goddesses, Hera, Aphrodite and Athene, was the most beautiful, and to indicate his decision by handing her a golden apple given to him for that purpose. Each goddess offered to bribe him and he succumbed to Aphrodite's bribe – that if he gave the apple to her he would win the most beautiful woman in the world. (This was Helen, wife of Menelaus, and supposedly, Paris, by stealing her from her husband, initiated the Trojan war.) However, Robert Graves suggests that the three women are actually the three aspects of the ancient triple goddess, to whom all apples already belonged, and that the goddess is awarding the apple of immortality to the shepherd.

Another story which he considers in a totally different light to the usual one is that of Andromeda's rescue from the sea-dragon by Perseus. This one is especially important because most scholars now accept that it is likely to have inspired, or at least influenced, the legend of St George killing the dragon, originating, as it does, in the same geographical area as both the contenders for the title of the historical St George. Graves deals with it quite summarily, saying:

> Andromeda's story has probably been deduced from a Palestinian icon of the sun-god Marduk, or his predecessor Bel, mounted on his white horse and killing the sea-monster Tiamat. In the same icon, the jewelled, naked Andromeda, standing chained to a rock, is Aphrodite, or Ishtar, or Astarte, the lecherous sea-goddess, 'ruler of men'. But she is not waiting to be rescued; Marduk has bound her there himself, after killing her emanation, Tiamat the sea-serpent, to prevent further mischief.

Above *The twentieth-century artist, M. C. Escher, chose the tail-biting dragon for his wood-engraving, and by doing so, helps to keep the ancient idea alive.*

Above *A painting by Piero della Francesca of St Michael (c.1469) holding the head of the slain dragon. Its body lies at his feet and appears rather small, perhaps to exaggerate the importance of St Michael.*

This interpretation does not tie in with the translation of *Enuma elish*, which makes it clear that Tiamat, creator of all, may give off emanations but cannot herself be an emanation. Certainly this ancient epic poem has been the source of later myths, but the question of who is misinterpreting what is still an unsettled subject of discussion among scholars. If, however, Robert Graves is right, his views strike a shattering blow at the very root of the romantic aspect of the dragon legend. The theme of the rescue of the innocent beauty from the horrendous beast appears throughout the art and literature of the West, and the suggestion that she is actually a witch, an enchantress of the worst kind, breathing out monsters to overcome the hero-figure, cuts the ground away from underneath it.

Sometimes the dragon was not so much accidentally misinterpreted as deliberately changed and adapted by later artists. For instance, Ernest Ingersoll says:

> ... it seems a fair inference that the aggressive Buddhist influence of the early centuries of that sect led Chinese artists to change the smooth, well-proportioned *Ch'ih-lung* of their forefathers ... into a sort of jungle python with the horrifying head and face characteristic of antique Buddhistic images of their demons.

It appears that, having somewhat tamed the ferocious Nagas and bent them to the service of the Buddha, Buddhist artists nevertheless found representations of the Chinese dragon too gentle, and occasionally felt the need to show him in another aspect, as a demon. The first Buddhist artists in China were probably aliens who, when they wished to show the dragon as demon, added cat-like attributes, because the people they were producing the images for saw few dangerous snakes but did see and fear tigers. Ingersoll says: 'The fully realised dragon, then, as we see it in bronzes or sprawled across a silken screen, is an invention of decorative artists striving, during the last 2,000 years, to embody a traditional but essentially foreign idea.'

But whatever the true intent behind early icons, and however much the later dragon may have been bastardized, it is still possible to understand a little more about his impact by considering the way his image has been used in art. His initial appeal is probably purely decorative. Visually, he is stunning. The Eastern dragon, whether voluptuous or ethereal, is always beautiful, the Western dragon, even when horrific, is sometimes beautiful and always dramatic. The serpentine shape has endless possibilities for design. It can slide along clouds or swirl in mist; it can encircle the whole world or a carved font; it can insinuate itself into the branches of a tree and pour down from the summit; it can explode like a sunburst on an imperial robe or entwine the legs of a knight's charger with its ominous coils. It is an early and widespread image. In *The Animal Style in South Russia and China*, M. Rostovtzeff, who was Professor of Ancient History and Archaeology at Yale University, attempts to trace the route taken by various artistic styles and influences which resulted in the material excavated in south Russia, and in so doing makes it clear that the dragon was an important symbol throughout the ancient world.

He says that the Scythians, who controlled south Russia from the eighth to the third centuries BC, used the dragon image which, by the fifth and fourth centuries BC had spread throughout central and eastern Russia. From the fourth century onwards, the Scythians were steadily overtaken and eventually conquered by a group of peoples called Sarmatians by the Greeks. During the Sarmatian period the dragon became the most frequently used animal symbol, together with the eagle-griffon (possibly related to the Garuda). The animal style in south Russia appears to have received influences from Persia, the southern Caucasus, Ionian Greece and the Greek colonies on the north shores of the Black Sea. But both the so-called Scythian and Sarmatian styles were already evolved by the time they reached south Russia, so where did they come from? Not, it appears, from Persia or Greece because although both had the dragon and both influenced south Russian art, Persia merely accepted the Near Eastern animal style with no modifications and Greece accepted it with only a few modifications. This implies that it may have come from the Near East, but Professor Rostovtzeff rules this out because he says that, although Assyria, Babylonia and Phoenicia certainly had the dragon, 'the Scythian animal style is more primitive, more vigorous, less than the animal style which reigned in the Near East in the first millenium BC'. A vigorous primitive style would be extremely unlikely to evolve from a more sophisticated one.

Professor Rostovtzeff suggests that the possible source of the style was China because the art of the Chou dynasty (c. 1125–250 BC) was flourishing at about the time that the animal style came to south Russia. And the dragon symbol was dominant in the art of the Chou dynasty.

There are still problems. For instance, it appears that the style flowered suddenly in China, with all its characteristics present, in other words, it did not evolve there. And further, both the Chinese eagle-griffin and the dragon appear to be Mesopotamian in style which brings the problem more or less full circle and leaves unanswered the question as to which came first, the Chinese dragon or the Mesopotamian dragon. Were they created independently or did they have a common source?

This brief and over-simplified summary hardly does justice to the

Above *The Japanese dragon is similar to the Chinese dragon, except that he has only three claws, as opposed to four, or five of an Imperial dragon. He is still a weatherlord, who must ascend into the sky to stir up the clouds before life-giving rain can fall (late seventeenth-century Japanese screen).*

Below *A thirteenth-century altar-piece by Margarito of Arezzo, showing the Virgin and Child enthroned, with scenes of the nativity and the lives of the saints. In the bottom right-hand corner, the dragon is shown swallowing St Margaret.*

Professor's meticulously researched book, but it does serve to give an indication of the many areas in which the dragon image was artistically important and the way in which influences flowed back and forth, modifying or enriching, but never obliterating it.

But wherever it originated, and whatever its degree of importance, in art it was always a symbol. In *Allegory and the Migration of Symbols*, Rudolf Wittkower says:

> There is a large body of cultural material, perhaps best subsumed under the vague terms 'symbols' and 'archetypal images', that we encounter through long periods of time and wide spaces, the origins of which are lost in the early dawn of history. The gammadion or swastika, the winged globe, the Tree of Life, the eagle and the snake, the Great Mother, the mythical hero as animal tamer, the dragon, and the totemistic fauna of animals and monsters all form part of this material. Scholars who tread this complex territory diverge widely, for the permutations of both type and meaning seem almost infinite.

One of the reasons for this great variety of meaning is that in the East, and to some extent in the pre-Christian West, the functions of particular deities were not clear-cut. Many philosophies teach that the force which creates and the force which destroys are one and the same, and that each has its place. Consequently one god can govern both aspects of the force, something almost incomprehensible to anyone raised in a society in which Christianity has polarized all forces into Good and Evil. Among Christians, it seems, only the alchemists understood the laws of change and fluctuation.

The difference between the Eastern and the Western dragon has already been stressed. And so it is not surprising that, for instance, on the robes and accoutrements of the Chinese mandarins he was the symbol of imperial power, the celestial dragon giving his blessing to the reign of the

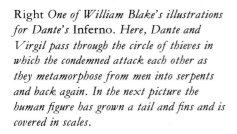

Right *One of William Blake's illustrations for Dante's* Inferno. *Here, Dante and Virgil pass through the circle of thieves in which the condemned attack each other as they metamorphose from men into serpents and back again. In the next picture the human figure has grown a tail and fins and is covered in scales.*

temporal ruler. Carved around the font in a Christian church, he symbolized the devil, from whose coils the infant was raised at baptism, freed from the danger into which he had been born to engage in his own personal fight against evil, with every possibility of winning.

Dragons figure in the emblems of several saints, to such an extent that even if a statue or picture has been defaced it is possible to recognize the saint by his or her relationship with the dragon. St George and St Michael are, of course, slaying it, and can be recognized one from another because St George is always on horseback whereas St Michael is on foot, winged, and often carrying the scales in which he weighs human souls. St Martha sprinkles her dragon with holy water, or leads him by her girdle. St Margaret bursts forth from the belly of the dragon that swallowed her. St John the Evangelist carries a chalice from which a tiny dragon can be seen to crawl. (St John was once furnished with poisoned communion wine but, because of his purity, neither he nor the communicants were harmed by it. God allowed the poison to escape in the form of a dragon.)

When regarding the dragon purely as a symbol, it is useful to remember that the number of heads with which he is endowed is significant. In *A Dictionary of Symbols*, J.E. Cirlot says: '. . . sometimes the dragon is depicted with a number of heads and its symbolism then becomes correspondingly unfavourable, given the regressive and involutive sense of all numerical increase.'

The symbolism of the dragon is given full reign in heraldry, in which every form, every colour and every stance has its specific meaning. True heraldry has been defined by Sir Anthony Wagner, Garter King of Arms, as '. . . the systematic use of hereditary devices centred on the shield', and the earliest known example of a shield with a personal device whose use by later generations can be traced is the blue shield charged with six golden lions of William Longespée, Earl of Salisbury, who died in 1225. But long before this personal device was used on shields, banners and battle standards, the dragon slain by Heracles appeared on his shield just as, centuries earlier, the dragon was the emblem of Marduk. However, these did not qualify as true heraldic devices because they do not appear to have been inherited by descendants.

The purple dragon ensign was the standard of the East Roman Emperors, and Edward Topsell (writing in 1607) describes dragon effigies borne by people called Draconerii which were obviously three-dimensional, hollow images, not unlike Chinese carp kites:

> And therefore when Constantius the Emperor entered into the City of Rome, his soldiers are said to bear, up upon the tops of their spears, Dragons gaping with wide mouths, and made fast with golden chains and pearl, the winde whistling in their throats, as if they had been alive, threatening destruction . . . .

Charles Gould mentions dragon ensigns of this type, saying

> Several nations, as the Persians, Parthians, Scythians, etc, bore dragons on their standards: whence the standards themselves were called dracones or dragons . . . . It is probable that the Normans borrowed this custom from the Parthians . . . but while the Roman dracones were, as we learn from Ammianus Marcellinus, figures of

Above *Even Leonardo da Vinci was excited by the dragon as a subject. Here, he shows the influence of classical stories on his art by creating a pen drawing of a seven-headed dragon.*

dragons painted in red on their flags, among the Persians and Parthians they were, like the Roman eagles, figures in relievo, so that the Romans were frequently deceived and took them for real dragons.

Whether or not anyone took them for real dragons, it is clear from these two descriptions that their function was the same as war paint or battle-cries to disturb, distract and frighten the enemy.

The dragon was the customary standard of the kings of England from the time of the conquest, and as such it figures in the Bayeux tapestry, but it did not form part of their armorial bearings. Henry VII took the red dragon of Cadwallader as one of his badges, claiming, as he did, uninterrupted descent from the early British kings Uther and Arthur. This was Y Ddraig Coch – the Red Dragon Dreadful of Wales, described as 'A dragon grete and grymme, full of fyre and eke venymme'. It was in Henry VII's reign that the dragon first appeared as a supporter of the shield bearing the royal arms, the red dragon on the dexter side with the white greyhound on the sinister side. As the *Encyclopaedia Britannica* says:

> In England before the Conquest the dragon was chief among the royal ensigns in war. Its origin, according to the legend preserved in the *Flores historiarum* was as follows: – 'Uther Pendragon, father of Arthur, had a vision of a flaming dragon in the sky, which his seers interpreted as meaning that he should come to the kingdom. When this happened after the death of his brother Aurelius he ordered two golden dragons to be fashioned, like those he had seen in the circle of the star, one of which he dedicated to the Cathedral of Winchester, the other he kept by him to be carried into battle.

Heraldry, or at least the use of personal insignia which preceded true heraldry, is probably the only area in which the Western dragon is not all bad. He is seen as symbolizing strength and power in battle and also as an omen of good fortune. In just such a way the Chinese dragon appeared in the sky as an omen of future kingship. The dragon, carried by Uther, was borrowed from him by the Anglo-Saxon kings. Britannica continues:

Above *Henry VII, being of Welsh descent, chose the red dragon and the white greyhound to support his Coat of Arms, shown here. Henry VIII retained the red dragon, but changed it to the sinister side.*

Left *William of Bruges, first Garter King of Arms, kneeling before St George, patron of the Order of the Garter, the earliest order of chivalry in Europe. Although the origins of the order are slightly obscure, it is generally believed that it was founded by Edward III on St George's Day, 1348 (Bruges' Garter Book, c.1430).*

The dragon ensign . . . borne before Richard I in 1191 when on crusade was that of the Dukes of Normandy – but even after the loss of Normandy the dragon was the battle standard of English kings. Not until the 20th century was it . . . restored as proper only to the British race of Uther Pendragon by its incorporation in the armorial bearings of the Prince of Wales.

Although in mythology and legend the dragon is acknowledged to take different forms, strictly and heraldically speaking a two-legged winged dragon is a wyverne (from the Saxon *wivere*, a serpent) and a wingless wyverne is a lindworm (Anglo-Saxon word for a legless dragon). In *Heraldry in History, Poetry and Romance* (1858), Ellen Millington discusses the wyverne, depicted with a child in its mouth, in the arms of the Visconti, Lords of Milan, which

Above *The baptism of Christ with the ascension and the resurrection of the dead in the background. On the left, a small figure of St George slays the dragon. Here St George is Christianity, overcoming the dragon of evil and death.*

Right *The fearsome dragon as a war machine. Roberto Valturio's* De re militari, *executed before 1462 at Rimini, shows this Arabian siege engine which uses the shape of the dragon both to attack and to frighten the enemy.*

... is said to commemorate the victory of a lord of that house over a fiery dragon ... which inhabited a cavern under the church of St Denis in that place. It is hardly possible not to think that the story of the dragon as well as its adoption in the coat-of-arms bears allusion rather to the dragon of paganism, expelled from the city, as it might seem, by the church built upon the site of the cave, in which too, by the rites of Holy Baptism, children especially were delivered from the power of Satan.

Medieval heraldry, especially, was strongly influenced by the Bestiaries, and typical heraldic beasts such as the lion, the griffin, the hart, the dragon and so on can all be found illustrated in the various Bestiaries which derived from the Greek *Physiologus*. Here, again, there was the possibility of misinterpretation, as was made clear in Sir William Segar's *Book of Royal Arms and Badges*, published in 1604. In it he discusses the panther, heraldically depicted as fire-breathing, saying that it is

... admired of all other beastes for the beauty of his skin, being spotted with variable colours; and beloved, and followed of them for the sweetness of his breath, that steameth forth of his nosethrills, and eares like smoke, which our paynters mistaking, corruptly doe make fire.

So the artists of the Bestiaries attempted to draw sweet breath, were misunderstood, and their panthers were adapted to breathe fierce flames. Similarly, perhaps, they intended to show the poisonous and corrupt breath of the anti-Christ dragon which, again, was misinterpreted, so that Western dragons are traditionally fire-breathing.

The dragon being slain by St George appears in the Regalia of the Order of the Garter, which is not only the earliest Order of Chivalry in England, but also the earliest in the whole of Europe. Although its origins are still slightly obscure, and it is not known, despite traditional stories, why the garter was chosen as the device or why *Hon Y Soit Qui Mal Y Pense* (Evil be to Him who Evil thinks) should have been chosen as the motto, it is generally agreed that the Order was founded by Edward III on St George's Day, 1348, and that St George was its patron saint. The 'lesser George', a pendant effigy of the dragon-slaying, was introduced as 'everyday wear' for the Knight during the reign of Henry VIII, and during the same reign the design of the ceremonial collar became formalized into 26 enamelled roses, with a gold knot between each, with the 'Great George', a larger jewelled pendant, depending from it.

The Celtic use of the word 'dragon' for 'chief', as in Uther Pendragon, may have preceded or resulted from the use of the dragon emblem as a standard. It appears that the title of 'dragon' was only bestowed in times of danger, and its use is undoubtedly the source of at least some dragon legends. In *Myth-land* (1886), F. Edward Hulme says:

There is a place in Berkshire called Dragon Hill, near Uffington, and the more famous White Horse Hill, that is in local legend the scene of the encounter between St George and the dragon; and for full confirmation a bare place is shown on the hillside where nothing will grow, because there the poisonous blood of the

116

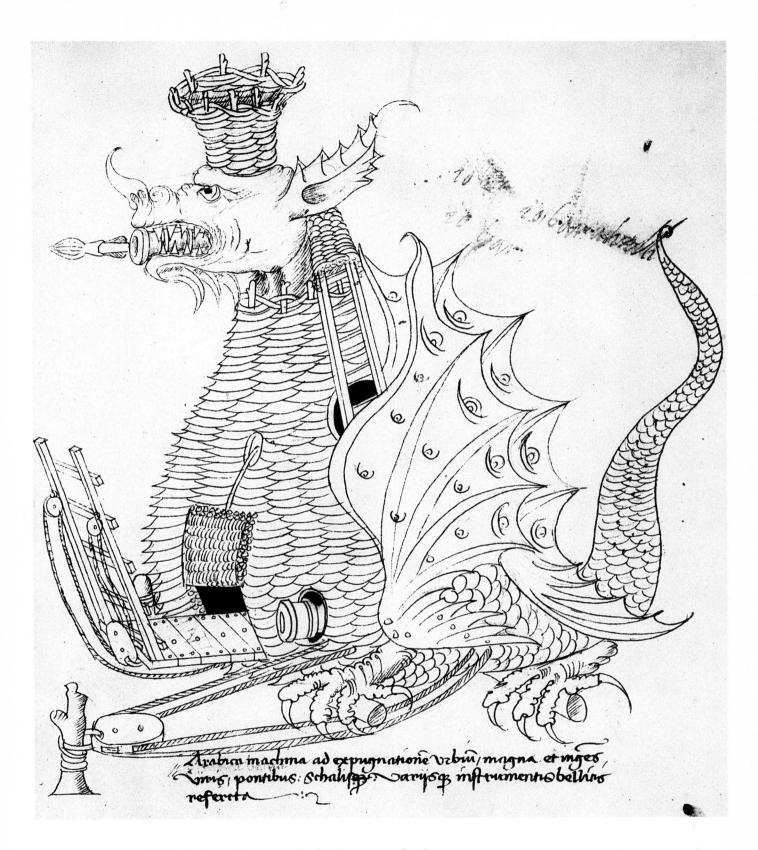

Arabica machina ad expugnatione vrbiu, magna et inges
oms, pontibus schalisq; varysq; instrumentis bellicis
referta :·:

creature was shed. We learn, however, in the Saxon annals, that
Cedric, the West-Saxon monarch, overthrew and slew here the
pen-dragon Naud, with five thousand of his men. The name of the
hill, therefore, commemorates this ancient victory; but the common
folk of the district, who knew nothing of pen-dragons, erroneously
ascribe the battle won there to the more familiar St George.

Slaying the Dragon

The slaying of the dragon is largely, although not exclusively, a Western phenomenon. In the East, and most particularly in China and Japan, the dragon was always respected, sometimes revered, and frequently courted for the rain and wisdom which were in his gift. In the West virtually the only dragon who was spared the hunt was the dragon as omen.

Strange phenomena traditionally attend the births of all great men. These strange phenomena, such as the star of Bethlehem, have taken various forms of which the dragon is only one, and the symbolism of this ominous dragon is the same in both East and West. A flight of one or more in the sky, usually at night and usually accompanied by a great light, promised the birth or the rise to power of a man of destiny. This man was always a leader, but not necessarily a ruler. He was as likely to wield spiritual as temporal power, and sometimes both. The dragon promised greatness and wisdom which, coming together in one man, gave him power over others. Wisdom was equated with goodness. A wise man could not be an evil one, although a merely clever man certainly could be. So the dragon did not attend the birth of every ruler or every man of power, only of those in which wisdom and power met.

In Britain the best-known dragon-augury was the vision of two golden dragons which appeared to Uther, father of King Arthur, as an assurance, so the augurers said, that he would rule. In Imperial China dragons attended the births of wise emperors and of sages, sometimes appearing in the Yellow River in full daylight, and a great azure dragon hovered briefly over the house where Confucius was about to be born.

The dragon as omen was never slain, and indeed could not be slain because he was a vision, a light in the sky, an apparition in the river. But the dragon in most other aspects was put to the sword for one reason or another. The significance of the slaying depends entirely upon what the dragon is seen to be – the Primal Waters; Darkness, the Dark and Unconscious side of man; the Force of Evil or the Devil himself; the Devourer, thief of immortality; the Alchemical Symbol for the *prima materia*; or the guardian of a hoard. And it is only through the meaning behind the slaying of the dragon, and the meaning behind the treasure hoard, that it is possible to glimpse the meaning of the dragon symbol.

The Dragon as Primal Waters, or as Chaos, was often killed as a part of the act of creation, sometimes so that its body could be used to form the structure of an ordered universe, and sometimes because it opposed the act and attempted to sabotage it. At this early stage, the ambivalent nature of the dragon was already apparent, and never more so than when it was synonymous with the Great Mother. Tiamat gave birth to all creation, and then turned against her progeny. The great cosmic dragon-serpent was set

Left This painting by Gustav Moreau of St George, depicts man's desire to conquer the lower for the sake of the higher. The maiden is shown praying, in a literally elevated position, while the halo around St George's head emphasizes that he can only succeed by the grace of God.

to bind the earth, tail in mouth, to keep it whole, but longed to break free and destroy it. The primal waters are the womb of life, but they are also flood and tempest, holocaust and inundation – the power to create and to destroy contained within one element and its symbol.

The symbolism of the Great Mother is an ancient and complex one. She is the triple goddess whose three aspects are as maiden, mother and hag. As maiden she is sacrificed to the male principle, which impregnates her, and as mother she brings forth. But as hag she is death, she is the underworld, and her womb is the grave. It is in this dark, chthonic aspect that she is most often identified with the dragon, with devouring death. Rebirth is the keynote. In most of the great religious systems and in all the mystery religions, spiritual rebirth can take place after physical death, but it can also take place during life, as a result of enlightenment, spontaneously received or induced by ritual.

In Christian baptism a man is symbolically born again 'of water and the spirit'. In the Greek mystery cults the novice was often led or directed into a symbolic death, underground, in the death-womb of the earth, where he was initiated into the deeper symbolism of the cult and then reborn, emerging into the light after an incarceration which often lasted three days. The image of the primal waters is a female image. The waters are impregnated, by the spirit or the wind, and bear life. The chthonic aspect of these waters is the female dragon, the image of death. In just such a way the snake is the chthonic aspect of the tree. The tree is life and it fruits above ground, the snake is death and lies curled in the tree's roots under the earth. But the snake, with its ability to cast its old skin, is also the

Right *The Wedding of St George by Dante Gabriel Rossetti. St George is the best-loved of the dragon slayers, easier to identify with than the archangel Michael. In this romantic representation, the emphasis is on the rescued princess and a strictly earthly marriage. Sterner interpreters of the story saw the lady as the Church, rescued from the dragon of paganism by staunch Christianity.*

symbol of rebirth and immortality. So, too, the Great Mother, even in her death aspect, is a womb from which comes new life. In the deepest sense, this dragon cannot be avoided. It will devour, but it will cast forth the enlightened man, just as the whale cast forth Jonah. The primal dragon must be overcome by the hero to ensure his spiritual survival.

In mythologies which are attached to refinements of cults such as these, the symbolism of dragon and hero can be extremely complex. The hero enters the womb of the dragon-mother in order to be reborn. When he clings in fear to the mother he is the dragon, and when at last he is reborn from the dragon-mother he is the conqueror of the dragon.

The most ancient of all mysteries apparent to man were the mysteries of birth and death, and almost every culture has assumed death to be a rebirth somewhere else. The Great Mother, creatrix and destroyer, by definition gave birth to everything. *Enuma elish* expressed this by showing that Tiamat bore gods, men and dragons. In the same way, the myth of the conflict between life and death, with rebirth as the goal, itself gave birth to the other aspects of dragon symbolism, whether reinterpreted, misinterpreted, elaborated upon or distorted by misunderstanding.

The Dragon as Darkness, the death of light, threatens the sun or creator. The fact that, in traditional mythology, the dragon was so often slain by a solar or sky god suggests that many of the early stories may have been attempting to explain fundamental natural phenomena, initially seen as the creative battle between chaos and order, and later as the recurring battle between light and dark. Each evening the dragon devoured the hero, and each morning the hero slew the dragon and rode in triumph across the sky. A more serious battle, and triumph, took place at the time of the winter solstice. Then the Sun, who could be seen to be progressively weakened by his repeated conflicts, was apparently threatened with total extinction, but overcame the danger, and as a direct result of winning such a victory became progressively stronger and more able to carry out his daily task of subduing the potentially engulfing dark.

Above *A Persian minature (1675)
depicting Bahram Gur shooting the dragon
with his bow and arrow.*

This view of the battle between light and dark, night and day, has been extended in all directions and has become the battle between winter and summer, ice and fire, the positive and negative aspects of life, drought and flood, and so on. It also has much in common with the ritual slaying of the corn god which symbolized the inevitable death of the ripe corn, from the ears of which would grow the new harvest. Ancient dragons were often regarded as female, the earth, the yin force – and ancient fertility rites played on the indivisibility of life and death, the symbolic impaling of the female by the male, or the spilling of the blood of the sacred king at the end of his year of office.

The symbolism of the reaper and the corn is fairly straightforward. Just as it must sometimes have seemed too much to hope that the sun would overcome the winter dark yet again, so it must sometimes have seemed impossible that the dead ears of harvested corn would give birth to the new crop upon which life depended. Accordingly, magical rites accompanied the reaping and great significance was attached both to the reaper and to his actions.

The Dragon as the Spirit of Evil existed in the early combat myths, but often had served a good purpose at the beginning, or was made to serve one by the conquering hero. The fertile but chaotic waters were tamed. But the two protagonists in the battle were polarized most sharply by formalized religion, and especially Christianity, which presented the battle as being between the wholly good and the wholly bad. Possibly the most significant difference between those who saw the dragon as one of two opposing but complementary forces, and those who saw the dragon as specifically evil, lies in their attitude to the creature's death. In the earlier myths, death was not seen as a permanent state, it was the conflict itself which was all-important and which created the essential energies of the universe. The sun rose, the sun set, the corn was cut and killed, the corn grew green again. Early cultures which, unlike the Chinese, believed in the necessity of slaying the dragon, most often saw it as a continuous and necessary process, literally a part of the rhythm of life. It was only when the dragon-side of the coin was presented as wholly evil that the death was seen as a final triumph, even by theologies which promised an after-life.

The Dragon as the Force of Evil was understood in various ways within that definition. Sometimes it was undifferentiated evil which was permanently in conflict with undifferentiated good. In Christian teaching it was often identified with the devil, or else with a very specific form of something seen to be evil – such as heresy or paganism. It was also often seen as the bad, or lower, side of man's own nature, which he must overcome in order to be whole.

In its demonic aspect, the dragon breathed fire and smoke and the stench of its breath was a hazard in itself. This was because, as an emissary of the devil, its mouth was like the mouth of hell, full of flames and sulphur, and to be devoured by this dragon was to be swallowed irrevocably into hellfire.

Some of the stories of the slaying of this dragon were written as allegory and were intended to be understood as such. Those which deal with the putting down of heresy or paganism by the power of the cross fall into that category. But many of the Christian stories were told, or elaborated, in an age when the devil and demons were believed to be physical realities, who could actually threaten and torment mankind, and this belief coloured many stories which present the dragon as an actual animal, physically real and mortal, who was motivated by demonic powers. In stories of this kind the importance of the iron lance wielded by the hero is always stressed. Iron, which was also used to impale vampires, was believed to be proof against the forces of evil. The dragon was destroyed not only because he was pierced through the throat, but because he was pierced by iron. The symbolism attached to iron stems from the fact that the first iron known to man was meteoritic in origin. It fell from the sky, from heaven, and therefore was holy and proof against the forces of hell.

But it is possible that the stories which presented the dragon as a physical emanation of the devil, being slain by a holy man on behalf of God, were over-simplifying the symbolism of the conflict. Certainly they overlooked the extraordinarily close relationship between slayer and slain, which has often been shown to be at least as close as that between Cain and Abel. Stories which present the battle as symbolic rather than literal, and as taking place often within the hero-figure himself, make the relationship clearer.

The dragon-slayer not infrequently took on the attributes of the dragon, and an echo of this can be seen in the adoption of the vanquished dragon as the emblem of the hero. The dragon, in this case, often represented basic physical energy, sometimes specifically sexual energy, put in bondage to the intellect. This dragon was slain and symbolically

Below Another story from the Persian Book of Kings, *which tells of Rustem killing the dragon as the second of his seven trials. Rustem's trials were said to symbolize the struggle between Iran and Turania. In pictures which show the horse helping the knight to defeat the dragon, it is possible to interpret all three as aspects of one man; the dragon as his lower nature, the horse as his physical body and energy, and the rider as his guiding intellect.*

eaten by the hero, that is, its energy was tamed and assimilated within the enlightened man. For instance, Siegfried tasted the blood of Fafnir and understood the language of the birds, or regained mastery over the lower forms of life that was lost by Adam in the Fall.

The Dragon as Devourer is slain by the hero to protect those he would devour, and he takes many forms. In his simplest form he is a man-eating animal, a predator, and it seems likely that at one time the name 'dragon' was applied to any dangerous animal of suitably daunting proportions. In this case, he was justifiably hunted to extinction by a breed of early chivalrous vermin-exterminators and his slaying was a brave, if prosaic, act for the benefit of humanity.

In mythological terms the Dragon as Devourer was more complicated than that. He did not simply devour the unwary, as a crocodile might, he demanded the sacrifice of numbers of youths and virgins. His demands increased steadily until only the highest possible sacrifice, the child of the king himself, would do. At this stage, traditionally, the hero-figure stepped in and slew the dragon. The king's child was saved, but enormous numbers of earlier victims were lost.

Going further into the symbolism of the myth it is possible to see this dragon as Time, relentlessly swallowing up youth, from whom not even the child of the highest temporal authority is immune. This devourer can only be overcome by an initiate, such as St George, who, because he is redeemed, has access to immortality and is therefore above and outside time. By symbolically overcoming time and death in front of her, the hero causes the enlightenment of the king's virgin daughter who stands for the soul in its purest and worthiest aspect, so that she too is redeemed and saved from the fate of the ignorant.

The idea that time is the thief of youth and life is an old one, and so is the idea that the subtle serpent, the death-symbol, stole mankind's immortality in the garden of Eden by persuading him to eat of the forbidden tree, while himself eating of the tree of life. This fall could only be redeemed by the death and resurrection of God himself who conquered death for the sake of mankind, and who, as has been seen, was sometimes actually identified with the serpent.

The Alchemical Dragon was the symbol of the dragon and slayer which the alchemists took for their own and used in their texts to help to disguise their true meaning. Although they were using a symbol which already existed, and not creating a new one, they probably helped to keep alive the story of the ritual slaying because whenever their lavishly illustrated texts fell into the hands of the uninitiated the words would have been read not as a recipe but as a story. They used the dragon in one of its earliest forms, as the *prima materia* of the universe, the base matter from which purer matter, the alchemical gold, was to be formed. And the mystical alchemists, especially, regarded the slayer, the slain and the sword as one. The adept who succeeded in transforming the base material to gold had slain his own dragon, which was also the cosmic dragon, and had risen within himself to a higher form of life, which nevertheless still contained the original dragon. The slain dragon was transmuted, not destroyed. (When considering how and why the dragon-myth eventually became attached to the Christian martyr, George, it may be worth bearing in mind that when Diocletian was persecuting and torturing the Christians, he was also persecuting and banishing the alchemists. The alchemical literature,

Below The sign of Sagittarius in an Islamic astrological treatise, c.1250. Sagittarius is usually depicted as a centaur shooting at the stars, but is here shown firing down the throat of the dragon on his own tail. The probable interpretation is that Sagittarius, whose chief attribute is ambition, is here overcoming his own lower nature as a prelude to spiritual advancement.

with its vivid illustrations of the slaying of a dragon by a hero-figure, was burnt or smuggled away alongside Christian literature. Without going so far as to say that the Christian George was in any way connected with the alchemists, it is possible to state that the alchemists were Christians.)

It has already been pointed out that the alchemical dragon is slain, in a sense, for the gold he guards, and throughout legend and myth it is for this reason that the Dragon as Guardian is always slain, to gain the treasure. Evil and degenerate dragons, like the dragon in *Beowulf*, guarded treasure they had found or stolen, guarded it for the sake of guarding it, and out of greed and malice took awful revenge on anyone who dared to take any of it. Traditionally it was the treasure of the dead, and it was guarded in tombs, caves and underground caverns. The treasure, usually gold, was of no value to the dead or to the dragon, and the whole operation was pointless and based on spite. But all this happened when the true meaning of the treasure, the dragon and the cave had been forgotten and the story degraded. The outward and worldly form taken by the treasure was almost always that of gold and pearls, and the symbolism of these two runs more or less parallel.

Gold has been regarded as medicinal for centuries. The pearl, too, held an important place in early medicine. Its powers were not unlike those of gold in that its virtues included prolonging youth, and it was supposed to be effective in treatment of cases of poisoning and diseases of the eye.

Both these treasures reached the world of medicine by way of the world of magic, but before they reached either they were archetypal symbols of metaphysical importance, connected with the sun and the moon. The symbolism of each, and especially of the pearl, is extremely complex and subtle, but they principally stand for 'truth' and 'life'. The truth, or knowledge or 'gnosis', is the spiritual truth for which every man must seek in order to find salvation and everlasting life. It is hidden and hard to find. The way to it is as strewn with obstacles as Christian's path in *A Pilgrim's Progress*, and it has a dreadful guardian who must be overcome if truth is to be attained and eternal life achieved. This is the dragon-serpent, the underworld, into which the adept must descend in his search.

The symbols of immortality are all there; the incorruptible gold, associated with the sun which sets to rise again; the lunar pearl, associated with the moon which wanes and dies and then waxes full again; and the serpent, symbol of death and resurrection. It is immortality that the Guardian Dragon holds.

So the 'treasure' guarded by the mythical dragon is life, even life everlasting. But there is an earlier treasure still. Although it has travelled a long way, the dragon is still 'the monster who holds back the waters'. In the Italian, Arabic and Hebrew languages the word for 'spring' is the same as the word for 'eye'. Springs are the eyes of the earth. An eye belongs in a head, and a head on a body. The serpent or dragon, with his glassy eye, coiled beneath a stone, was the form and shape chosen. His eyes were springs of water, life-giving water which yet could become destructive flood. The dragon had to be propitiated so that he would not become enraged and inundate the land, and also so that he would continue to bestow his priceless treasure on mankind.

The water-guarding dragon has come to symbolize immortality. The slain dragon always rises again. The very idea of the serpent-dragon is immortal. Even today, when symbolism is not a major part of our

Above *An illustration from a French version of the Apocalypse. The woman, to whom was given the wings of an eagle, and the five men (representing mankind), fight the dragon that St Michael cast down to Earth after a struggle in heaven. Rev. 12:13–17.*

language, the dragon exists as an idea. He cannot be forgotten.

But after the question 'what does the dragon mean to man' comes 'where did the dragon-shape originate'? Whatever may be said about the meaning of the archetypal dragon-serpent, what is still uncertain is why all dragons should take much the same shape and form. If the dragon does not, and never did, exist in a literal form then where does the vision of a powerful reptile come from. There is only one really satisfactory answer and it has not yet been proved to be possible. It is the theory which has been discussed for generations, and which has most recently been put forward by Dr Carl Sagan, that we still retain a dim race memory of a time when our proto-human ancestors were in conflict with the great reptiles whose primeval shapes and world-wide power haunt us still.

Above *An Egyptian papyrus painting from the Book of the Dead of Lady Cheritwebeshet. Here, Seth leans over the prow of the sun-boat to spear Apophis, the sun-god's eternal enemy, thus ensuring that there will be a new dawn.*

Right *In Chinese water festivals dragon boats were raced in imitation of dragon fights. The hope was to precipitate a real dragon fight and thus bring on the precious rain. The dragon image has travelled and changed, but still survives, especially connected with water, as with this dragon on the prow of an ex-Jesus College barge.*

126

Bibliography

Anderson, M. D. *Drama and Imagery in British Churches* (CUP 1963)
Animal Carvings in British Churches (CUP, Cambridge 1938)

Ashmole, Elias *Theatrum Chymicum Britannicum* (OUP, Oxford 1967)

Ashton, John *Curious Creatures in Zoology* (J. C. Nimmo, London 1890; Gale Research Co., Detroit 1968)

Attenborough, David *Zoo Quest for a Dragon* (University of London Press, London 1965)

Attwater, Donald *Dictionary of Saints* (Penguin Books, Harmondsworth 1970)

Bayley, Harold *The Lost Language of Symbolism* (William & Northgate, London 1912)

Beowulf – trans. Michael Alexander (Penguin Classics 1973)

Bett, Henry *English Legends* (Batsford, London 1952)

Bhattacharya, Sukumari *The Indian Theogony* (CUP, Cambridge 1970)

Binyon, Laurence *The Flight of the Dragon* (John Murray, London 1911)

Bose, Hampden C. du *The Dragon, Image and Demon* (London 1886)

Brandon, S. G. F. *Creation Legends of the Ancient Near East* (Hodder & Stoughton, London 1963)

Bricker, Charles *A History of Cartography* (Thames & Hudson, London 1969)

Brinton, Daniel G. *The Myths of the New World* (Leypoldt & Holt, New York 1868; 3rd edition, Philadelphia 1896)

Budge, E. A. W. *The Gods of the Egyptians* (2 vols) (Methuen, London 1904)

Carus, Dr Paul *The History of the Devil and the Idea of Evil* (Kegan Paul, London 1900)

Cirlot, J. E. *Dictionary of Symbols* – trans. Jack Sage (Routledge, Kegan Paul, London 1972)

Coe, Michael D. *The Maya* (Penguin, Harmondsworth 1971)

Collins, Arthur *Symbolism of Animals and Birds Represented in English Church Architecture* (Pitmans, London 1913)

Conze, E. *Buddhist Thought in India* (Allen & Unwin, London 1962)

Coomaraswamy, A. K. *The Aims of Indian Art* (Broad Campden, 1908)

Costello, Peter *In Search of Lake Monsters* (Garnstone Press, London 1974; Berkley Publishing, New York 1975)

Donatus, Sister Mary *Beasts and Birds in the Lives of Irish Saints* (Philadelphia 1934)

Douglas, Norman *Birds and Beasts of the Greek Anthology* (Minerva Press, London 1974)

Eliade, Mircea *Images and Symbols* (Harvill Press, London 1961)

Elliot Smith, G. *The Migration of Early Culture* (Longmans, London 1919)

Epic of Gilgamesh – trans. N. K. Sandars (Penguin, Harmondsworth 1970)

Fergusson, J. *Tree and Serpent Worship* (W. H. Allen, London 1868)

Figuier, Guillaume Louis *World Before the Deluge* (Cassell, London 1891)

Fox-Davies, A. C. *Complete Guide to Heraldry* (London 1909)

Frankfort, Henri *Cylinder Seals* (Macmillan, London 1939)
Kingship and the Gods (University of Chicago Press, 1948)

Frazer, Sir J. G. *Folk-lore in the Old Testament* (Macmillan, London 1923; Hart Publishing Co., New York 1975)

George, Wilma *Animals and Maps* (Secker & Warburg, London 1969)

Gesner, Conrad *Historia Animalum* (Frankfurt 1617)

Goldsmith, Elizabeth *Ancient Pagan Symbols* (Putnam, New York 1929)

Gordon, E. O. *Saint George* (Swan Sonnenschein & Co, London 1907)

Gould, Charles *Mythical Monsters* (W. H. Allen, London 1886, reprinted Gale Research Co., Detroit 1969)

Gould, M. M. *Sea Serpents* (London 1886)

Graves, Robert *Greek Myths* (Penguin, Harmondsworth 1969)

Guillaume Le Clerc de Normandie *The Bestiary* – trans. G. C. Druce (Headley Bros, Ashford, Kent 1936)

Guillim, John *Display of Heraldry* (London 1724)

Heidel, Alexander *The Babylonian Genesis* (CUP, Cambridge 1951)

Henderson, Joseph L. *Ancient Myths and Modern Man*, Essay included in *Man and His Symbols* Edition C. J. Jung (Aldus, London 1975)

Herodotus *The Histories* – trans. A. de Selincourt (Penguin 1971)

Heylin, Peter *The Historie of St George of Cappadocia* (London 1659)

Holmyard, E. J. *Alchemy* (Penguin, Harmondsworth 1968)

Homer *The Iliad* – trans. E. V. Rieu (Penguin, Harmondsworth 1950)

Hooke, S. H. *Middle Eastern Mythology* (Penguin, Harmondsworth 1963)
Myth and Ritual (OUP, London 1933)

Hopkins, A. J. *Alchemy, Child of Greek Philosophy* (Columbia University Press, New York 1934)

Hulme, F. Edward *Myth-land* (Sampson & Low, London 1886)

Ingersoll, Ernest *Dragons & Dragon Lore* (Gale Research Co., Detroit 1968)

Jameson, Anna Brownell *Sacred and Legendary Art* (Longmans, London 1905)

Jastrow, Morris *Aspects of Religious Belief and Practice in Babylonia and Assyria* (Lippincott, Philadelphia & London 1911)

Jewitt, Llewellyn *The Dragon of Wantley and the Family of Moore* (London, 1887)

Joly, H. L. *Legend in Japanese Art* (Kegan Paul, London 1967)

Jung, C. G. *Alchemical Studies* (Bollingen Foundation, New York 1967)
The Archetypes and the Collective Unconscious (Routledge, London 1959; Bollingen Foundation, New York 1967)

Kramer, S. N. *Sumerian Mythology* (Memoirs of the American Philosophical Society, Philadelphia 1944)

Leach, Maria *Funk and Wagnall's Standard Dictionary of Folklore, Mythology and Legend* (New English Library, London 1975; Funk and Wagnall, New York 1972)

Lindholm, Dan *Stave Churches in Norway* (Steiner Press, London 1969)

Lum, P. B. *Fabulous Beasts* (Thames & Hudson, London 1952)

Mandeville, Sir John *The Bodley Version of Mandevilles Travels* (OUP, Oxford 1962)

Marcus, G. J. *St George of England* (Williams & Norgate, London 1929)

Michell, John *The View Over Atlantis* (Garnstone Press, London 1974)

Millington, Ellen I. *Heraldry in History, Poetry and Romance* (London 1858)

Nicholson, Irene *Mexican and Central American Mythology* (Hamlyn 1967)

Nuttall, Zelia *The Fundamental Principles of Old and New World Civilisations* (Vol 2 of the Archaeological and Ethnological Papers of the Peabody Museum, Harvard 1901)

Okakura, Kakasu *The Awakening of Japan* (Century Co, New York 1904)

Oldham, C. G. *The Sun and the Serpent* (Constable, London 1905)

Pauwels, Louis & Bergier, Jacques *The Dawn of Magic* – trans. Rollo Myers (Panther, London 1964)

Pepler, H. D. C. *Concerning Dragons* (Privately printed, London 1916)

Polo, Marco *The Description of the World* – trans. A. C. Moole & Paul Polliott (Routledge & Sons, London 1938)

Richardson, Maurice *The Fascination of Reptiles* (Deutsch, London 1972; Hill and Wang, New York 1972)

Rostovtzeff, Professor M. *The Animal Style in South Russia and China* (Princeton Monograph No. 14, 1929; Hacker Art Books, New York 1975)

Sagan, Dr Carl *The Dragons of Eden: speculations on the evolution of human intelligence* (Hodder & Stoughton, London 1978; Random House, New York 1978)

Taylor, Frank Sherwood *The Alchemists* (Paladin, London 1976; Henry Schumann, New York 1949)

Thompson, C. J. S. *The Mystery and Lore of Monsters* (London 1930)

Topsell, Edward *The Historie of Foure-Footed Beastes and Serpents and Insects* (Frank Cass, London 1967; W. J. Johnson, 1973)

Vinycomb, John *Fictitious and Symbolic Creatures in Art* (Chapman & Hall, London 1906; Gale Research Co., Detroit 1969)

Visser, Marinus Willem de *The Dragon in China and Japan* (Amsterdam 1858)

Vogel, J. P. *Indian Serpent Lore* (London 1926)

Waddell, Helen *Beasts and Saints* (Constable, London 1934)

Wendt, Herbert *Before the Deluge* – trans. by Richard & Clara Winston (Paladin, London 1970)

Werner, E. T. C. and Hyman Kublin *A Dictionary of Chinese Mythology* (Julian Press Inc, New York 1961)
Myths and Legends of China (Harrap, London 1922; Arno Press, New York)

White, T. H. *The Book of Beasts* (Jonathan Cape, London 1969; Humanities Press, New Jersey 1969)

Whittick, Arnold *Symbols, Signs and their Meaning* (Leonard Hill, London 1960)

Williams, C. A. S. *Outlines of Chinese Symbolism and Art Motives* (Charles E. Tuttle Co, Inc., Tokyo, Japan 1974)

Wiseman, D. J. *Cylinder Seals of Western Asia* (Batchworth Press, London 1959)

Wittkower, Rudolf *Allegory and the Migration of Symbols* (Thames & Hudson, London 1977; Westview Press, Colorado 1977)

Zimmer, H. *The Art of Indian Asia* (Pantheon Books, New York 1955)
Myths and Symbols in Indian Art and Civilization ed. J. Campbell (Pantheon Books, New York 1962)

Index

Numbers in italics refer to illustrations

Aeëtes, King of Colchis 31–2
Alchemical Dragon 66–77, 119, 125
alchemists' flasks *66, 75*
alligators *79*, 84, 91–3
Ananta (1000-headed cobra), Vishnu lying on *44*
Andromeda *see* Perseus
Anthropos, three manifestations of the *70*
Apollo 27, *27*, 28
Apophis 9, *9*, 13, 23, *23*, 24, 66, 79, *126*
Apsu 20, *21*
astronomy and astrology *84*, 84–5
Athene (or Minerva) 30, 31, 32, *32*, 86, 109

Bahram Gur, King *107, 122*
Beowulf 98, 100–1, 107, 125
Bestiaries *33*, 48–9, *51*, 80, 81, 116
The Bible 14–16, *15*, 46–8, 49
The Book of Kings 106, 123
Borgia World Map (1435) *81*
boundary stones, Babylonian/Assyrian *15, 20*
Buddha, Buddhism *12*, 41, 42–3, *45*, 110

Cadmus, King 30–1, *31*
Chih-wen, Chinese dragons 40, *40*
Chinese Imperial Dragon 41, *42*
Chinese New Year Dragon 38–9
Christ, baptism of *116*
church architecture, early European 49–51, *50*
City of London Coat of Arms *114*
Codex Marcianus 10
Codex Troana *11*
Codex 2801 83–4
Coiling Dragon, Chinese 39
Conyers, Sir John 101
creation myths 14–16, *15*, 17, 22, 57
crocodiles *13, 91*, 91–3, *97*
crucified serpent *16*
cyclops 89

Dan Ayido Hwedo, heavenly serpent 12
Dan gbwe, earth serpent 12
Daniel and the lions *103*
Darkness, the Dragon as 119, 121–2
Delphic Oracle 9, 27, 28, 30
Desceliers, Pierre, world maps of 80, 81
Devourer, the Dragon as 119, 124
dinosaurs 89, 90
double-headed dragons *57, 60–1, 121*
doves, symbolism of 49, *51*
Drachenfels, dragon legends of 90, 99
Draco, constellation 38, 84, 85
Draco volans (flying lizard) *94*, 95–6
Draconerii 113
dragon eggs 36
dragon ensigns 113–17
Dragon Hexagram 76
dragon-horse or Chinese Yellow Dragon 39, 40
Dragon Lantern, Japanese 41
Dragon of Wantley 101, 103–6, *105*
dragon paths (*lung-mei*) 76

Ebstorf World Map 80, 81
Echidne 28, 29
elephants *14, 26*, 33
Enlil, father of the gods 18, 19, 22
Enuma elish (Babylonian epic poem) 19–20, *21*, 110, 121
Ethiopian MS, St George from *54*
Eurystheus, King 28, *28*, 29

Fafnir, dragon 98, 99, *99, 101*, 124
Force of Evil, the Dragon as 119, 122
fossil (dragon) bones 89–90, 106
Frazer, Sir James 14–15
Fu-ts'ang lung, Chinese dragon 41

Garden of Eden, serpent of 14–16, *15*, 46, 93
Garuda, Hindu divine bird 37, 43
Genoese World Map (1451) *78*
George of Cappadocia 52, 54
Gilgamesh 22, *22*, 32
globes, terrestrial and celestial 84–5, *85*
Gnostics 14, 16, *16*
Gould, Charles 44–5, 88, 89, 113–14
Great Mother, symbolism of 119, 120–1
green dragon *66, 67*
Guardian, the Dragon as 9, 119, 125–6
Gushtasp, Prince *34*

Henry VII, King 114, *115*
Henry VIII, King *115*, 116
Hera 27, 28, 109
Heracles (or Hercules) 28, *28*, 29, *29, 30*, 85, 103–4
heraldry 113–17
Hereford World Map 80, 81
Hesperides, Garden of the 28, 29
The Historie of Four-Footed Beastes (Topsell) 86, *86–7*
Holy Ghost, dragon fertilized by *69*
horoscopes *84*, 85
Horus *14*, 24
Humbaba, dragon 22
Hydra of Lerna 9, 28, *29*

I Ching 40–1, 76
Icelandic *Eddas* 10, 88, 98
Illuyankas, dragon 24
Indra 10, *11*, 23
Ishtar Gate, Babylon *17, 18*

Japanese ivory netsuke *19*
Jason and the Golden Fleece 31–2, *32*
Jonah and the whale *33*, 121

Kenabeek, serpents *64*
Komodo dragon *95*, 96
Kukulcan, Mayan 58, 60, *61, 63*
Kur, dragon 18, 19, 22

Labbu, sea-dragon 18
Ladon, dragon *28*, 28–9, 85
Lahmu and Lahamu 20
Laidley Worm of Lambton 101, 102–3
lake monsters 60–5, *62*, 91, 97
lindworm (legless dragon) 115
Linton Worm 101–2, 108
lizards *see Draco volans*; Komodo dragon
Loch Ness Monster 61, *62*

mandarin robe embroidered with dragon *42*
Mandeville, Sir John 81–3, 102
maps *78*, 78–81, *81, 83–4, 97*
Marco Polo *79*, 83, 84
Marduk 18, 19, 20–1, *21*, 109
mask, Aztec wood and mosaic *57*
Mercurial dragon 71–2, 73, *73*, 74, *77*
Midgard Snake/Serpent 10, 14, 88, *102*
More of More-hall 104–6, *105*
Moses exorcizing the dragon *35*
Musrussu dragon, Babylonian *18, 20*

Nagas, Indian water deities 9, *10, 12*, 14, *14*, 37, 38, 41–3, *45*, 110
Nibelung Saga (*Nibelungenlied*) 51, 90, 98, 99
Ninurta, god-hero 18, 19, *24*
Norse mythology 14, 98–9, *101*
Norwegian stave churches 49–51, *50, 101*

Ophites, Gnostic serpent-worshippers 16
Order of the Garter *115*, 116
Osiris 23

Ogopogo, lake dragon 61–2
Ouroboros, tail-biting dragon *10*, 66, 69–71, *70*, 77

panthers *33*, 116
pearl, symbolism of *36*, 37–9, *38, 39*, 125
Perseus and Andromeda *6–7*, 32–3, 54, 109
plumed serpents 13, 43, 57–60, *58–60, 63*
prima materia 66, 66–7, 69–71, 74
Primal Waters, the Dragon as 119
Python 9, 12, 27, *27*, 28, 93
  African 94, *94*
  Indian rock 94, *94*

Quetzalcoatl 13, 43, *58*, 58–60, *60*

Ra (Re), sun-god *9*, 23
  Cat of *23*
Red Dragon Dreadful of Wales 114, *115*
Rig Veda 10
Rome, dragon inhabiting marshes *88, 93*
Rustem *122*

St George 9, 14, 20, 22, 37, *49*, 51–2, *54*, 54–5, *57*, 76, 113, *114, 115*, 116–17, *116, 118, 120*
St Margaret *55, 111*, 113
St Martha 55, 76
St Michael 47, 49, 51, *53*, 55, 76, *110*, 113, *121, 125*
St Servatius seal showing dragon-goddess *16*
St Simeon Stylites 55–6
seals *16, 36*
  Babylonian cylinder *21*, 21–2
Sebek, Egyptian crocodile god *13*
serpent-dragons 8–16, 41–2, 46–7, 57–60
Seth (or Set) *14, 23*, 24, *126*
seven-headed dragons *16, 47*, 113
Shen-lung or Chinese Spiritual Dragon 39, 41
Siegfried 90, *99, 99*, 124
Sigurd 99, *101*
Slimey Slim, lake dragon 62
Sockburne Dragon 101
Somerville, William de 101–2, 108
'Spanish landing in America' (du Bry) *65*
snakes 93–4

Tatsu, Japanese dragon 41
Temple of the Warriors, Chichen Itza 60, *63*
Theogony (Hesiod) 25–6
Tiamat 19–21, *21*, 22, 109–10, 119
T'ien lung or Chinese Celestial Dragon 39, 41
Ti-lung or Chinese Dragon of the Earth 41
Titans 25, *25*
Topiltzin, King 59–60
Topsell, Edward 86–7, *86–7, 92*, 96, 106, 113
Tree of Life 14–16, 49, 112
Typhon, monster 25–7, 28, 29

Uraeus *14*
Uther Pendragon 114, *115*, 116, 119

Vietnamese dragons *38, 40*
Viking ship burial site, carved head from *50*
Visconti, Lords of Milan 115–16
Vishnu 43, *44*

weather-lord dragons, Eastern *36*, 37
Whidah, Dahomey, serpent cult at 12
wyverne (2-legged winged dragon) 115–16

yin and yang, Chinese symbol of *38, 39, 39, 67*

Zeus 21, *25*, 25–7, 30
Zodiac, signs of the *15, 19*, 45
Zu, storm bird 18